More *Lefton China*

Ruth McCarthy

I0809245

Schiffer Publishing Ltd
4880 Lower Valley Road, Atglen, PA 19310 USA

Dedication

This book is dedicated to the hundreds of wonderful Lefton collectors I have met this past year, not only in person, but on the awesome world-wide internet! Isn't it wonderful living in the age of computers? It opens a whole new world of adventure in Lefton collecting! I thank you so much for all of your wonderful cards, letters, and email this past year since my first book was published. That in itself is what has prompted me to write this second book. My hope is to add new insight, information and enjoyment in your Lefton collecting.

Disclaimer

"Lefton China" is a registered trademark of the Lefton China Company. The Lefton China Company did not authorize this book nor furnish or approve of any of the information contained therein. This book is derived from the author's independent research.

Library of Congress Catalog Card Number: 99-066893

Designed by Bonnie M. Hensley
Type set in University Roman/Zapf Humanist

ISBN: 0-7643-1028-3
Printed in China
1 2 3 4

Published by Schiffer Publishing Ltd.
4880 Lower Valley Road
Atglen, PA 19310
Phone: (610) 593-1777; Fax: (610) 593-2002
E-mail: Schifferbk@aol.com
Please visit our website catalog at **www.schifferbooks.com**

In Europe, Schiffer books are distributed by Bushwood Books
6 Marksbury Avenue Kew Gardens
Surrey TW9 4JF England
Phone: 44 (0)208-392-8585; Fax: 44 (0)208-392-9876
E-mail: Bushwd@aol.com

This book may be purchased from the publisher.
Include $3.95 for shipping. Please try your bookstore first.
We are interested in hearing from authors with book ideas on related subjects.
You may write for a free printed catalog.

Contents

Acknowledgements 4
History 5
Identifying Marks 6
Introduction 9
Lefton Patterns, Styles, and Series 10
Pricing 16
Americana (Rose) 17
Angels 21
Series #3332 26
Series #489 29
Series #6224 32
Series #808 36
Animals and Birds 39
Banks 44
Bells 46
Bloomer Girls 48
Candle Holders 55
Canister Sets and Cookie Jars 57
Christmas 62
Coffee, Tea, Sugar and Creamers 68
Covered Dishes/Boxes 73
Decorative Items 76
Dishes, Tidbits, and Compotes 82
Dresser Sets and Perfumes 86
Figurines 88
Girls 88
Ladies 93
Guys 98
Boy Series #2300 102
Couples 105
Fruit Fantasia 108
Green Holly (Holly Berry) 110
Hands 115
Head Vases 119
Jam Jars 124
Miss Priss 127
Mushroom Forest 131
Pearlized/Opalescent Items 136
Pitchers and Bowls 140
Planters 143
Birds and Animals 143
Figural Planters 145
Miscellaneous Planters 148
Salt and Pepper Shakers 151
Saucers, Cups and Snack Sets 157
Smoking Related Items 161
Vases 165
Wall Hangings and Pockets 171
Bibliography 176

Acknowledgements

A heartfelt thank you, with love, to the following people:

My husband Dan McCarthy, who never seems to tire of taking the pictures for my books, and for all his love, support, encouragement, patience, and help, which makes it possible for me to continue to write books on my Lefton China collection. Many, many hours of intensive picture taking were included in his already overloaded schedule this past year, along with numerous conversations and much time spent with our film developer.

All of our children and grandchildren who have always been there for me with their love, support and encouragement.

Fran Harris and Steve Bellamy at Snap Shots Inc. in Sandusky, Ohio, who worked with us closely and developed the photographs for this book.

Linda and Jim Batt, who possess a large collection of Christmas items as well as some of the rare pieces. They have been so kind in sending me pictures to use in my books.

Sara Selander, from Minnesota, who has given me much encouragement and supplied me with Lefton pieces from her collection.

Meri Stalh, who came to Ohio from Illinois to visit with me, share her old Lefton catalogs and talk about Lefton. Never enough time, is there Meri?

Cindy and Mike Schneider, my special friends, who gave me that gentle push and encouragement to write my first Lefton book and have continued to support me in writing this second one.

All of the hundreds of Lefton collectors I have met on the Internet who have supplied me with bits and pieces of information I have been able to put together in hopes it will give new insight to the Lefton collector.

Stuart Brown, who not only supplied me with pictures of his own collection of Lefton China, but spent many hours doing research from his collection of the old Lefton catalogs. Only by working with Stuart have I been able to add so much new information in this book.

As many collectors have, Stuart started his collection of Lefton because of a mini ewer in pink porcelain Forget Me Not flowers, given to him by a relative. He has collected Lefton actively for about four years and favors Lefton's decorative items, especially the pink and white porcelain pieces with raised flowers, and the glass vases. Stuart's other interests in Lefton include their catalogs because of the wonderful information available in them. He actively hunts for Lefton at local estate sales, antique malls, garage sales, and flea markets, and his collection has grown from the initial single item in Forget Me Nots to over 1000 items at present. Stuart is also interested in photography as a hobby, and deals in computers as a profession.

History

The Lefton China Company was founded in 1941 by George Zoltan Lefton in Chicago, Illinois and is still operating there today. Mr. Lefton was born in Hungary and made his living there by designing and manufacturing sportswear. While in Hungary, his hobby was collecting fine china, and after coming to the United States in 1939 he began shaping ideas for his own ceramic business. After WWII, Mr. Lefton began importing ceramic giftware from the Orient. Although Japan has always been the major source for manufacturing Lefton China, manufacturing was expanded to other countries starting in the 1970s. China, Taiwan, Malaysia, Sri Lanka and Mexico were in this expansion, as well as Italy and England. These are the factory stickers we see on Lefton China today. Lefton China is a wholesale business, and their products can be found in fine retail gift shops all over the country. The Company has showrooms in several cities in the United States, including Chicago, New York, Atlanta, Boston, Columbus, Dallas, Denver , Detroit, Kansas City, Miami, Minneapolis and Oklahoma City. Due to the excellent quality and wide variety of styles, patterns and series, Lefton China will be in great demand for many years to come.

Mr. George Zoltan Lefton passed away on May 29,1996. I've often wondered if Mr. Lefton had any idea when he started his company that his name and fine quality products would reach so far into the future.

Mike Schneider wrote the following in his book *The Complete Cookie Jar Book* on Mr. George Lefton and his legacy.

> In recent years some import companies, Enesco for example, have considerably upgraded the quality of their ceramics to the point where there is little doubt they will become the collectibles of tomorrow. Lefton hasn't because there was no need to!

What a fine tribute that is to George Zoltan Lefton and the continuing Lefton China Company.

Identifying Marks

Most Lefton items are marked in some way with fired-on trademarks or paper labels (referred to in this book as stamps and stickers), and numbers. Letters preceding the numbers are the factory's abbreviated identification marks and suffix letters may mean a variety of things such as right, left, the color of the item, small or large, to name a few. Some pieces have the year of copyright on them. Any or all of these trademarks are usually found on the bottom of the piece, and aid in dating and identifying Lefton China. I have been able to contact other import companies, and like Lefton, it seems that most of these companies in their early stages of production were not all that concerned about keeping records on the dating of their products. Thus, there is no way to be *completely* accurate in the dating of Lefton stamps and stickers used on their products.

I have had many letters, calls and emails concerning some of the markings and dates on Lefton items this past year. It seems collectors are searching for more information on the subject of markings and dates. For instance, the "Made In Occupied Japan" stamp used between 1945 and 1953 because it was "required by law during General MacArthur's administration of post-war Japan", is not on some of the items produced during that time. Instead, on many of those pieces there is just a large red sticker (Lefton' s Exclusive Japan, 1946-53) or the multi colored stamp (Lefton China, with a crown, Hand Painted, 1946-53), or both. The question is why, if it was a *law* during that time period, is there no "Made In Occupied Japan" stamp on all of these items? In Lefton's 1980 Collectors Guide it just says that items made in that time frame were "also labeled" Made in Occupied Japan. Those are key words; they could also mean " besides other markings" and "labeled" perhaps meaning paper labels? If paper labels were used they probably would, after that length of time, come off. All the pieces I own or have ever seen have the "Made In Occupied Japan" stamp, so I have nothing to back up this theory. Hopefully by continued search into the older Lefton catalogs, more information will be found for my next book.

The following paragraphs have been written to help answer questions from the mail I have received, and to give you Lefton collectors some "food for thought".

There is a three-piece perfume set found in this book in the "Dresser Sets and Perfumes" chapter, page 86. This item is found in Lefton's 1980 Collector's Guide, which says there were 4788 pieces produced in pink and white from 1955-1957. In other collectors' books on Lefton, it has been said that the large red sticker was used from 1946-1953 and the stamp used from 1946-1950. So it looks like both of these markings were used longer than originally thought.

Another example found in the 1980 Lefton Collector's Guide is a beautiful covered swan candy dish (there is a picture of it in the "Covered Dishes/Boxes" chapter of this book, page 74). It says that only 900 of these were produced in 1954. I believe this to be a rare piece due to the number of them produced. There is no number on this dish, just the stamp said to have been used from 1946 to 1950. So there again, this stamp had to have been used until at least 1954.

In the chapter on Figurines, on page 94, there is a lady with three markings on the bottom. The stamp on the left was thought to have been used from 1946-1950, the stamp on the right from 1950 to at least 1970, and the larger sticker from 1946 to 1953. But the date, and I'm sure it is the date, is 1955. Here again, this shows us that these markings were used for a longer period of time than originally thought. Another interesting discovery is the color of the stamp on the right. It is red and not black. I have at this time been unable to find any information on this red stamp.

I have tried to mention all identifying marks found on each piece in this book, and the majority of these items were made in Japan during the 1950s, '60s and '70s, with very few from the '80s and '90s. Considering that so many different and unusual markings have been found, I wanted to show as many of them as possible. The black sticker, to my knowledge, has been found on only Christmas items. Since it is identical to the red sticker it would seem that this black sticker was used in the same time frame, from 1960-1983. Most of the items I have with this stamp date in the 1970s.

The mark "Limited Edition" in the early years of Lefton manufacturing was not on items as such. If there was just a small number of any item manufactured it was possibly due to the loss or destruction of some of the molds. I have seen very few items with "Limited Edition" on them, the Pinkie and Blue Boy figurines being the most popular.

Very little information has been found on the ESD Canadian Imports that so many people ask about, concerning dating. Research is still being done on that as well as some of the newer stickers from Taiwan, China, Malaysia, Sri Lanka, Mexico, England and Italy.

While searching for Lefton, you'll find pieces with one, all, or none of these identifying marks. How do you know if the piece you have is really Lefton if there are no marks or numbers to go by? There will be times when you won't know for certain. Paper labels are easily washed or worn off and have even been known to be lifted off and attached to items that are not Lefton. Therefore, *please* check items with paper labels very closely.

A good example of this is found in my first book in the chapter on Figurines. I have shown four different pieces that I believed to be Lefton. My knowledge was limited at that time and I went by the stickers that were on these pieces. I have been told since that these four pieces were in fact made by Napco. Items in question are a little girl with Feeding Time #1110, Little Mother #AH1D, Little Seamstress #AH901 and Monday Wash #AH1H. If this has caused confusion to anyone, I am truly sorry.

I have found pieces that have no markings, but since they have been part of a set or part of my existing collection, they can be identified by that alone. There are identical pieces with different numbers as well as identical numbers on different pieces. Some have different factory codes, but the same number. Identifying Lefton pieces can be difficult, but isn't this all part of the exciting challenge in finding that Lefton item?

The majority of the dates used for the following stickers (paper labels) were derived from the second Lefton book written by Loretta DeLosier. Dating of a variety of the fired-on stamps used on Lefton will be found through out this book. Please keep in mind that the dating on some or all of these paper labels and stamps may be off by a few years, as was explained previously.

The largest and oldest of the red stickers with a silver or gold trim, Lefton's Exclusives Japan. 1946 to 1953.

This sticker is a new find, not found in any other book. It is large like the one used from 1946 to 1953, except with different wording. (Lefton's Reg. U.S. Pat. Off. Exclusives Japan). I would think, due to the "Reg. U.S. Pat. Off" wording, that this sticker was used in the same time frame as the small one with the same wording, which was used from 1953-71.

Medium size red sticker with gold or silver trim. Lefton's Reg. U.S. Pat. Off. Exclusives Japan. 1953-1971.

Medium size red sticker with gold trim, Lefton Trademark Exclusives Japan. 1960-1983.

Medium size black sticker with a larger border of gold trim, Lefton Trade Mark Exclusives Japan, may have been used during the same time frame as the red sticker with same lettering, 1960-1983. This sticker appears mostly on Christmas items.

Medium size sticker, red with gold trim, Lefton Trademark Exclusives Japan,(® over the "on" of Lefton). 1962-1990.

Round black sticker with silver lettering and trim, Hand Blown Glass Works, Lefton's Japan. These stickers are found on most of Lefton's older glass pieces.

Although Japan has always been the major place of manufacturing for Lefton China, during the 1970s manufacturing was expanded to other countries . The following stickers are shown from these countries, and all of these have the ® over the "on" of Lefton. The starting date was in the mid-1970s, and to my knowledge they are still being used today. I have many items with these stickers that are dated up until 1998.

Medium size red sticker with gold trim, Lefton Trademark Exclusives China.

Medium size red sticker with gold trim, Lefton Trademark Exclusives Malaysia.

Medium size red sticker with gold or silver trim, Lefton Trademark Exclusives Taiwan.

Medium size red sticker with silver trim, Lefton Taiwan.

Medium size red sticker with gold trim, Lefton Trademark Exclusives Sri Lanka.

Very small, black oval sticker with Japan in the center in silver and silver trim. This sticker is found on many of the older Lefton items along with Lefton's identifying markings.

Small oval red sticker with Made In Japan in the center in silver with silver trim. This sticker is also found on many of Lefton's older items along with their own identifying markings.

Introduction

Almost everyone today has a collection of some kind, and more and more people are falling in love with the look and feel of Lefton China. There are so very many different patterns, sets and series to choose from! Cookie jar collectors love the quality of Lefton, as do collectors of dinnerware, people and animal figurines, planters and head vases. I've heard from people all over the world concerning their Lefton collections, including Japan. One would think Lefton would be easily found in that country as that is where so much of it is produced. From the letters and emails I have received, that isn't the case; it seems to be rather scarce in that country.

Any type of collection can be expensive, but it doesn't have to be if you know where to look for the items. Flea markets, garage sales, dim-lit antique mall basements and estate auctions are still and hopefully will always continue to have bargains for the collector and dealer. Other great places to find what you are looking for in Lefton are the auctions on the internet. People from all over the world have Lefton to sell or trade and you don't even have to leave your home.

My most serious collection today, of course, is Lefton China. The many angel series, head vases and older pieces are among my favorite. I started my collection several years ago, after my mother passed away. She had four lovely items and they were left to me. There was a bloomer girl, an angel, a vase and a planter, all with red stickers, letters and numbers on the bottom of them. Of course, at that time I had no idea what those markings were, but after several years of research and searching for items, I am finally coming to understand some of them. Today, my collection is over 2000 pieces strong, and I'm still adding.

The greatest thing about a collection, no matter what it consists of, is the challenge of looking for and finding that one special piece—the heart-pounding thrill you get when you see that item you've been looking for. You know, the one that's part of a set, or the rare piece, or that one with the unusual mark or sticker. There it is, peeking out of a dirty old box, on a shelf behind other items, or right there in front of you, and you wonder why no one else saw it. But no, they didn't, you did, and now it's yours to buy, take home, and cherish.

Depending on your type of collection, it's nice to have items for everyday use. With Lefton you have that choice. Figurines and wall hangings are in every room of our house, three of my banks collect coins, animals are in groupings in china cabinets or on small table tops, and angels are on bathroom shelves, bedroom window sills and on top of my kitchen cabinets. Many of my planters and vases contain plants both real and fake, from ivy to tulips. Picture frames contain pictures, candle holders grip candles and a few of the salt and pepper shakers hold their intended products. Cookie jars sometimes contain what they were made for but most often have in them those small bits of things one doesn't know where else to put! Several sets of canisters are packed away for future use, as a change every few months is nice and the canisters made by Lefton go with most any color scheme.

Finding whole sets of dinnerware with plates, cups and saucers in excellent condition is almost unheard of due to every day usage. The teapots, coffee pots, sugars, creamers and snack sets were normally used only occasionally, therefore surviving longer. Very old items with delicate flowers are also difficult to find in *perfect* condition. Difficult perhaps, but not impossible. There are still many perfect pieces of the older Lefton out there, and with diligent searching and patience, can be located.

People have written to me concerning the cleaning of Lefton items. With the thin and delicate arms, legs, wings and flowers there is always the fear of breaking something. I have found that Lefton cleaning can be fun. I use several types of small brushes such as a soft tooth brush, the tiny little brush that comes with a man's electric shaver, and the one that comes with a toothbrush-type handle that is used for cleaning between teeth. That one is handy for tiny crevices, as it is shaped like a Christmas tree. Soaking in hot or warm water with dish soap or shampoo for a short time when the item is extremely dirty works wonders. Rinse and apply more soap, and the little brush of your choosing then removes all of the built-up dirt. Most Lefton is delicate, but not so much so one needs to be afraid to give it a good bath. I've bought many Lefton pieces on the internet auctions this past year and so many times they arrive needing a thorough cleaning. Several items were described to have nicks or chips on them and, in fact, after cleaning, I discovered they were actually mint! It's always such a pleasure to see just what is under all that dirt.

There are Lefton collectors throughout the country wishing to buy, sell or trade pieces and the quarterly newsletter on Lefton China is an excellent way to do this. You can join the National Society of Lefton Collectors by simply writing to the National Society of Lefton Collectors, 1101Polk Street, Bedford, Iowa 50833, or calling 712-523-2289. This news letter is very informative, with updated news and pictures on the Lefton world, a classified section, personal stories, and much more.

I am always happy to hear from others concerning their Lefton collections and can be reached by phone, 419-668-0738, or by e-mail, ruth@accnorwalk.com. Your input on my books, suggestions, and ideas are always welcome. Sharing thoughts and information is what these books are all about.

Lefton Patterns, Styles, and Series

Below you will find a list of patterns, styles, series, and collectibles that were produced by the Lefton China Company. This list was derived by searching many of the Lefton catalogs from the middle 1950s and into the 1990s. It is not yet a complete list but it gives the Lefton collector more insight as to just how much Lefton there really is on the secondary market today. I find it quite overwhelming, as I had no idea when I wrote my first book that there were so many different patterns and series. In searching through the Lefton catalogs it has been found that because there are so many patterns, not all of them can be identified with a name. In the older catalogs, some items have names while others do not. One example is the flowers. Some catalogs identify the flower pattern with a name such as Heirloom Rose or Luscious Lilac, while others simply call it rose or lilac.

Beside each listing is a brief description of as many as were found and the date of the Lefton catalog each was found in. Perhaps this information along with stamp and sticker dates, will help you in dating your Lefton collection.

I again want to thank Stuart Brown for all the time and effort he has contributed this past year in helping me to compile this list and its information!

AMERICANA ROSE

(See Chapter on Americana Rose)

AMERICAN CHILDREN

Collectible boys and girls in matte finish found in an undated Lefton catalog from the 1950s.

ANDORRA

These are little boy and girl figurines with an optional wood base, #224 to #230. Found in Lefton's 1974-75 Holiday book.

ANTIQUE IVORY BISQUE

APPLE BLOSSOM

AVIARY

A collection of bisque birds. Owl, Grouse, Eagle, Penguin, Crane and the Bobwhite with optional wood bases seen in Lefton's 1986 catalog.

BARNYARD FRIENDS

Animal collection with separate wood base, including cats, dogs, mice, chickens, pigs, wolves, raccoons and geese seen in Lefton's 1986 catalog.

BERRIES AND BUTTERFLIES

An English Import, this is a kitchen table piece pattern of white porcelain with hand painted red strawberries, white strawberry blossoms, green leaves and colorful butterflies. Listed are a teapot, two-tier tidbit, cream and sugar, sandwich tray, square dish, round bonbon dish and square bonbon dish. #741 to #748. Seen in the 1986 Lefton catalog.

BERRY HARVEST

BISQUE POINSETTIA

Lefton's Holiday Book, 1974-75, pictures a large line of this pattern from #218 to #223 and #8024 to #8088. Included pieces are vases, pin box, basket, ashtray in three shapes, candleholder, oil lamp, covered candy box, pitcher with bowl, sprinkler planter and bell. Lovely white bisque with applied red poinsettias and green leaves, some with gold trim.

BOUTIQUE, BISQUE

Found in the 1974-75 Holiday Book by Lefton, this pattern is shown in pink, blue and yellow background with clusters of hand painted flowers. Includes vases, planters, picture frames, dishes, toothbrush holders, sprinkling cans, pitcher and bowl sets, hand mirrors, cups and covered small boxes.

BOUTIQUE, PORCELAIN

This pattern was found in Lefton's 1986 catalog with the following description. "The delicate buds of the blooming Narcissus, the purple velvet of the regal Violette, the willowy sprigs of the Impatience cluster...all are captured in the exquisite floral patterns of Lefton' s exclusive porcelain Boutique Line. Beautiful bud vases, dainty pin boxes, lovely little picture frames are all adorned in meticulous hand painted detail". Another flower included in this line of Boutique was Pink Dogwood, with items consisting of cups and saucers, mugs, bells, pitcher and bowls, salt and pepper shakers, dishes and thimbles.

BLACK CHINTZ

BLACK VELVET

BLUE ASTER

BLUE BIRD

This is one of Lefton's highly collectible patterns today. This adorable Bluebird is found in an undated Lefton catalog from the 1950s, mostly in the #280 range. Fifteen items were pictured, including a wall pocket, wall plaque, teapot, cookie jar, baby set, jam jar, pitcher, milk mug, bank, planter, cheese tray, egg cup, salt and pepper shakers, sugar and creamer, and spoon rest with salt shaker.

In the 1965 catalog, only three items were pictured. The musical teapot, salt and pepper shakers and the baby set (a cup and bowl), #3552.

BLUE GRAPE

BLUE PAISLEY

Dinnerware and table accessories were featured on the cover of the 1964 Lefton catalog. Items shown included teapot, sugar and creamer sets, dish with handle, jam jar, compote, candy box, plates, nested ashtrays, round ashtray, egg cup, cigarette urn with ashtrays, bone dishes in two sizes, snack set, one and two tray tidbits, nappy, teabag holder, and salt and pepper shakers.

BLUE PLUM

BLUE ROSE

BOSSIE THE COW

In Lefton's 1974 catalog, six kitchen items are shown including a pitcher, butter dish, mug, sugar and creamer, salt and pepper shakers and a jam jar.

BRITISH

Figurines of British gentleman.

BROWN HERITAGE, FLORAL

In an undated Lefton catalog from the 1950s, numbering mostly in the #1800 range, there are ten items shown including plates, sugar and creamer, snack set, sandwich plate with handle, two tier tidbit tray, salt and pepper shakers, compote, teapot and a single tidbit tray.

Lefton's 1964 catalog pictures twenty items including #1264 tumble up, #468 candy box with lid, #051 pitcher, which was discontinued, #062 coffee pot, #055 sugar and creamer, #476 two cup teapot, #068 salt and pepper and several types of vases.

Included in Lefton's 1967-68 catalog are a pitcher, sugar and creamer, coffee pot, snack set, salt and pepper shakers, sugar and creamer, several types of vases, compote, bone dish, jam jar, tid bit trays, pitcher and bowl, plates and candy box.

The 1986 Lefton catalog shows twelve items numbering in the 04150 range, including coffee pot, sugar and creamer, plates, candy dishes, plates, salt and pepper shakers, but vases and a cake plate. As you can see by the number of catalogs this pattern appears in, it was and still is quite popular.

BROWN HERITAGE, FRUIT

In an undated Lefton catalog from the 1950s ten items are shown, including plates, cream and sugar, snack set, sandwich with handle, one and two tier tidbit trays, salt and pepper shakers, compote and teapot.

CABBAGE CUTIES

In Lefton's 1964 catalog, this gal was called Cissy Cabbage. There are seven items pictured, numbering in the 2120 range. Included are cookie jar, teapot, sugar and creamer, an 8" dish, salt and pepper shakers and a spoon rest.

CHEF BOY

CHRISTMAS BOW

Found in Lefton's Holiday catalog from 1974-75, #7742 to #7751, this pattern is white glossy porcelain with green and red holly berries and leaves, and a large applied red bow. Items shown include covered candy boxes, candle holder, bell, basket, sleigh, creamer and sugar, pitcher and bowl, and a three-compartment dish.

CHRISTMAS HOLLY

CHRISTY

CLASSIC ELEGANCE

Pictured in Lefton's 1967-68 catalog, this is an unusual rare and lovely pattern showing only six items of bowls and dishes, numbering from 4805 to 4810.

CLIP ONS

This collection consists of birds and butterflies with little clips attached to the back to clip on gift packages. Found in Lefton's 1986 catalog.

COLONIAL

Figurines of men, women and children from that time period.

COSMOS

Nine items, numbering in the 1070's, are pictured in Lefton's undated catalog from the 1950s. This is possibly one of Lefton's oldest patterns and is highly sought after by Lefton collectors. Items include a bonbon dish with handle, compote, candy box, snack set (tea and toast set), creamer and sugar, plates, salt and pepper shakers and a coffee pot.

COTILLION

COUNTRY CHARM

Eighteen pieces are shown in Lefton's 1967-68 catalog in two color schemes—white with a blue rooster and yellow with a green rooster. This is a kitchen pattern, #4602 to 4619, consisting of the following pieces: canister set, cookie jar, salt and pepper shakers, mugs, teapot, and cream and sugar.

COUNTRY GARDEN

There are four items shown in Lefton's 1974 catalog. Canister set #5930, oval platter #6199, cake plate #6198 and cup and saucer #6197.

COUNTRY SIDE

Collection of English Glassware, decorated with hand painted lace and flowers. Tidbits, plates and dishes are shown in 1986 Lefton catalog.

COUNTRY SQUIRE

CREATURES OF MYTH

Collection of white bisque Unicorns and Pegasus in several different poses and some are musical. Found in Lefton's 1986 catalog.

CRIMSON ROSE

CUDDLES

DAINTY MISS

In Lefton's undated catalog from the 1950s there are seven items. #322 sugar and creamer, #321 teapot, #040 cookie jar, #323 marmalade, #648 tea bag holder, #935 cup and saucer, #439 salt and pepper and #325 spoon rest and shaker.

DAISYTIME

DANCING LEAVES

"Kitchen Line" is Lefton's description on this pattern in their 1974 catalog, showing thirteen pieces from #7279 to #7310. Included are cookie jar, canister set, oval tray, compote, two-compartment dish, pitcher and bowl, egg plate, soup tureen, salt and pepper shakers, jam jar, napkin holder, butter dish and spoon rest.

DECEMBER HOLLY

DELLA ROBBIA

This pattern is found in the 1967-68 Lefton catalog. Twenty items are shown, numbering in the 4200s, 4100s, 1900s and others. Included are a fruit pyramid, salt and pepper shakers, sugar and creamer, oval platter, teapot, lavabo set, jam jar, plates, cookie jars, canister sets, two, three and five compartment dishes, relish tray, candy box, compote, and cake plate.

DIMITY ROSE

In the 1974 Lefton catalog, six items are shown numbering in the 6300's. Included are jam jar, teapot, vases, candy box and two sizes of pitcher and bowl sets.

DOGWOOD

DOLL HOUSE

Series by Marika found in the 1974-75 Holiday Book and consisting of bisque pixies, children, and story doll figurines.

DUSTY ROSE

DUTCH BLUE

Lefton's 1967-68 catalog shows sixteen pieces of this pattern, numbering in the 3900s and 3600's. This pattern has a garlic crusher which is a rare piece for Lefton. Other items shown are canister set, cookie jar, lavabo set, teapot, spice set with wood rack, sugar and creamer, jam jar, instant coffee jar, butter and cheese dishes, mug, egg tray, salt and peppers, double spoon rest and egg cup.

DUTCH GIRL AND BOY

EARLY AMERICAN ROOSTER

Numbering in the 1020s and 2100s, seventeen items are shown in a basket weave pattern with a chicken on a "nest". Found in Lefton's 1964 catalog, items include teapot, sugar and creamer, cookie jar, canister set, jam jar, salt box, match box, candy box, bread tray, tidbit dish, double dish, salt and pepper shakers, spoon rest, and teabag holder.

EASTERN ELEGANCE

EASTERN STAR

ELEGANT ROSE

ELEGANT VIOLET

ELF HEAD

There are only two items pictured in Lefton's 1967-68 catalog and both are shown as discontinued. #3970 sugar and creamer and #3973 teapot. I would consider these to be rather rare for that reason.

EMPRESS

Bone china roses with separate wood bases in light yellow, dark yellow, red, and pink. Lefton's 1986 catalog shows these along with "in blossom" flowers such as Magnolias, White Dogwood and Pink Dogwood.

ENGLISH HOLLY

ENGLISH HOLLYBERRY

White bone china with gold trim and painted red and green holly berries and leaves. The 1974-75 Lefton Holiday book shows just four pieces of this pattern. Teapot, plate, cup and saucer, and mug. Very similar to the Yuletide Hollyberry with the exception of fewer holly berries. Numbers are 520, 9039, 9038 and 001.

ESPRESSO

FESTIVAL

With hand painted grape clusters and vines, there are fifteen pieces of this pattern pictured in the 1967-68 Lefton catalog. All number in the 2600s except for the coffee pot, which is #2935. Other items included are a two tier-tidbit tray, plates, cream and sugar, jam jar, teapot, salt and pepper shakers, candy dishes, snack set, bone dishes and an eight-piece coaster set.

FIESTA

Kitchen line in a yellowish basket weave background with orange fruit, shown in Lefton's 1973 catalog. Numbering in the 5200s, there are five items shown.

FLEUR de LIS

FLORAL BISQUE BOUQUET

FLORAL BOUQUET

23 items of this pattern are found in Lefton's 1974 catalog, numbering in the 7100s, 7200s and 7300s. Pieces shown include a seventeen-piece coffee set, four types of jam jars, candy box, vases, ashtray set, pin boxes, candy dishes, soap dish, two sizes of pitcher and bowl sets, and a bell.

FLORAL BUTTERFLY

This pattern of white floral basket weave with butterfly handles is shown in Lefton's 1974 catalog. Canister set, #7530 and cookie jar, #7531.

FLORAL CHINTZ

With multiple types of flowers in an all-over chintz-like pattern, eleven pieces were found in Lefton's 1974 catalog, numbering in the 8000s. Items include a teapot, creamer and sugar, cup and saucer, plates, pitcher and bowl sets in three sizes, three types of nappy dishes, candy box, and compote.

FLORENTIA FLORA

This pattern was "inspired by the spring flowers along the Arno River and in the beautiful Renaissance gardens of Florence". Showing are plates, vases, covered boxes, bells, dishes and serving tray. White porcelain with very large colorful flowers, this is a lovely pattern. Numbering is from 00101 to 00119. Shown in Lefton's 1993 catalog.

FLOWER GARDEN

Lefton's 1974-75 Holiday Book shows canister sets, cookie jars and soup tureens in this pattern, #308 to #310, in yellow and pink.

FORGET ME NOTS

Some of the very oldest Lefton pieces were pink glossy porcelain with lovely applied pink and blue Forget Me Not flowers. These flowers mainly appeared on vases and planters.

FRENCH PROVINCIAL

Men, women and children figurines dressed in that time period.

FRENCH ROSE

In Lefton's 1967-68 catalog, forty items of this pattern are shown, numbering in the 3400s, 2600s and 3300s. Pictured items include a teapot, cream and sugar, cup and saucer, candle holders, jam jar, plates, match box, cigarette urn with ashtrays, salt and pepper shakers, nappy dish, pitcher and bowl, soap dish, lipstick holder, toothbrush holder, covered jars, vases, ring holders, purse planter, denture boxes, and pin boxes.

FRUIT BASKET

FRUIT FANTASIA

(See Chapter on Fruit Fantasia)

FRUITS OF ITALY

Twelve items of this pattern are shown in Lefton' s 1964 catalog, numbering in the 600s, 1200s and 11000s. All-over mixed fruit relief in low tone colors. Items shown include sugar and creamer, coffee pot, pitcher, cookie jar, two and three compartment dishes, trays, mug, tidbit tray, compote, jam jar, and salt and pepper shakers.

GAME BIRD

A collection of game birds including Bobwhites, California Quails, Pheasants, Peacocks, Canada Geese, sea gulls, and several types of ducks—including Canvasback, Widgeon, and Loon —are shown in Lefton's 1986 catalog.

GARDEN BOUQUET

GAY NINETIES

Figurines of women of that time period.

GINGHAM

There are forty items shown, numbering in the 3200s and 3300s in Lefton's 1964 catalog. This pattern was produced in three color combinations. Tan and apricot, purple and blue/grey and tan and misty green. Items included are coffee pot, salt and pepper shakers, cream and sugar, cup and saucer, jam jar, plates, mug, egg cup, and cookie jar.

GOLDEN LAUREL

GOLDEN LEAF

GOLDEN ROSE

GOLDEN TREE

GOLDEN WHEAT

GRAPE

Thirteen pieces of this grape pattern are shown in Lefton's 1964 catalog with varying numbers. Items shown include cookie jar, teapot, sugar and creamer, pitcher in two sizes, tray, measuring set, dishes, jam jar, plates, and candy box.

GREEN HERITAGE, FLORAL

Shown in Lefton's 1986 catalog, the numbers started with 01000 to 04000. Pictured are cake plates, bud vases, teapot, cup and saucer, two-tier tidbit tray, pitcher with tumbler, compote, pitcher and bowl, candy dishes, coffee pot, sugar and creamer, salt and pepper and Hors d'Oeuvre set.

This pattern is also found in Lefton's 1964 catalog including the tumble up, tidbit trays, vases, compote, snack set, plates, coffee pot, sugar and creamer, salt and pepper, jam jar, and a two-cup coffee pot.

GREEN HERITAGE, FRUIT

This pattern was pictured in several of Lefton's catalogs, but not referred to as "fruit".

GREEN HOLLY

(See chapter on Green Holly)

GREEN ORCHARD

HARLEQUIN

HARVEST PANSY

This kitchen pattern, with white basket weave background with pansies, is found in Lefton's 1974 catalog. There are five items shown with numbers in the 7900s, including a canister set, napkin holder, pitcher and bowl, cookie jar, and soup tureen.

HEAVENLY ROSE

Possibly one of the oldest Lefton serving patterns, there are fourteen items found in an undated Lefton catalog from the 1950s with some numbers in the 100s. Included are plates, cream and sugar, snack set, compote in two sizes, cup and saucer, salt and pepper shakers, teapot, bonbon dish, sandwich plate with handle, a cigarette set, and bone dishes.

HEIRLOOM ELEGANCE

HEIRLOOM ROSE

Pictured in Lefton's 1964 catalog are a candy dish, #1377 and a cup and saucer, #1076.

HOLIDAY PORCELAIN

Found in Lefton's 1974-75 Holiday catalog, this pattern is very similar to the White Holly with the exception of being smooth, compared to the "ridges" in the White Holly pattern. It is white shiny porcelain with small red and green holly berries and leaves, with gold trim. Items number from 7940 to 7956. Pieces shown are pitcher with bowl, two sizes, bud vases, candy box, bell, candleholder, nappy dish, jam jar/spoon, teapot, sugar and creamer, cups and saucers, plates, two-tier tidbits, and compote.

HOLLY BERRY

HOLLY GARLAND

HONEY BEE

HOT POPPY

ICE PINK BISQUE

Planters, vases, and candy dishes can be found in this decorative pattern in an undated 1950s Lefton catalog. Shown are seventeen pieces numbering in the 1000s and 1100s.

IMPATIENCE

White glossy porcelain with hand painted Impatience flowers. Included are bud vases, baskets, bells, pin boxes, leaf shaped bonbon dish, and pitcher with bowl, all pictured in Lefton's 1986 catalog.

ITALIAN ALABASTER

A collection of hinged-top trinket boxes; square, round, and egg-shaped; in pink, white, and lavender; with an assortment of hand painted flowers, shown in Lefton's 1986 catalog.

ITALIAN ROMANCE

LILAC CHINTZ

Twenty items are shown on this pattern in the 1964 Lefton catalog, numbering mainly in the 690s and 700s. Included are plates, cup and saucer, sugar and creamer, teapot, tidbit tray, shack set, compote, bone dish, egg cup, nested ashtrays, salt and peppers, jam jar, candy boxes, teabag holder, and cigarette urn with ashtrays.

LILY OF THE VALLEY

These applied flowers appeared on many of Lefton' s older items.

LITTLE ADORABLES (Limited Edition)

Found in Lefton's 1974-75 Holiday book, showing six figurines of little children, two on a base. All are #326. It says that there were only 720 pieces of each produced, which is what makes them a true limited edition.

LITTLE FRIENDS

Collection of little bisque girls in 18 poses measuring 3" to 4" high. There are three numbered sets of six pictured in Lefton's 1986 catalog. #04894, #03218, and #03222.

LUSCIOUS LILAC

MAGNOLIA

MARDI GRAS

MILK CHINA

MINIATURES

A collection of animals, birds and figurines ranging from sizes 1" to 3". An assortment of the miniature birds is found in Lefton's 1986 catalog.

MISS PRISS

(See Chapter on Miss Priss)

MISTY ROSE

MOSS ROSE

MR. TOODLES

Highly collectible Mr. Toodles is a white puppy dog in kitchen items and found in Lefton's 1964 catalog. There are nine items shown numbering in the 3200s and all pieces were discontinued, including a child's set, sugar and creamer, teapot, butter dish, egg cup, and planters in two different poses.

MUSHROOM FOREST

(See Chapter on Mushroom Forest)

MUSHROOM HOUSE

NEST EGG COLLECTION

A collection of different types of bisque birds found in Lefton's 1986 catalog. Beautiful detail with applied flowers and brilliant colors.

ONLY A ROSE

This pattern was called the "Red Rose" line by Lefton in their undated catalog from the 1950s, showing eight items and numbering 380 to 420. Included items are round ashtrays, perfume set, and five different types of vases.

ORIENTAL

Figurines of Spanish, Japanese and Chinese people.

PAISLEY FANTASIA

There are eighteen items shown in Lefton's 1974 catalog, numbering in the 6700s and 6800s and including plates, cream and sugar, coffee pot, tidbit trays, compote, three different sizes of pitcher and bowls, candy boxes, vases, bell, teabag holder, and pin boxes.

PIERROT

A collection of glossy porcelain clowns, hand painted black and white with gold trim, shown in Lefton's 1986 catalog.

PEAR N APPLE

Kitchen line pictured in Lefton's 1967-68 catalog. Eighteen items are shown, numbering in the 4100s, 3700s and 4300s, including dishes, oil lamp, butter dish, mug, lox and bagel dish, salt and pepper shakers, candy box, instant coffee jar, jam jar, two types of cookie jars, sugar and creamer, teapot, and two types of canister sets. In the 1974 catalog, #3755 canister set is shown.

PEARL LUSTER

Opalescent type figurines, planters and banks. (See chapter on Pearl Luster)

PINECONE

PINK AND BLUE DAISY

PINK CLOVER

PINK DOGWOOD

This is a lovely pattern referred to in the 1993 catalog as Heritage. Very similar in style to the Green and Brown Heritage floral pattern. Shown are bud vases, candle holders, pitcher with tumbler (or tumble up, as they are sometimes called), pitchers with bowls in two sizes, bonbon dishes, coffee pot, cream and sugar, three types of cups and saucers, teapot, two sizes of plates, cake plate and salt and pepper shakers. This pattern appears to be a white background with pink dogwood flowers and gold trim.

POPPY

PROVINCIAL

Figurines of men, women, and children of that time period.

ROMANCE

ROSE CHINTZ

RUSTIC DAISY

Lefton's 1967-68 catalog pictures eighteen items with numbers in the 4100s and 3800s. Included are two- and four-compartment dishes, plates, cream and sugar, cup and saucer, teapot, jam jar, instant coffee with spoon in two different sizes, cookie jar, and canister set.

SHASTA DAISY

SILVER WHEAT

Dinnerware numbering in the 2100s, such as plates, cups and saucers, cream and sugar, coffee pot and snack sets are found in Lefton's 1964 catalog.

SPRING BOUQUET

Numbering in the 4580s and 4590s, there are twelve items shown in Lefton's 1967-68 catalog including a pitcher, salt and pepper shakers, teapot, pitcher and bowl, cup and saucer, coffee pot, jam jar, three different shapes of nappy dishes, and plates.

SPRINGTIME

STRAWBERRY HARVEST

SUNFLOWER

SWEET STRAWBERRY

An English import of dinnerware found in Lefton' s 1986 catalog.

SWEET VIOLETS

Practically every serving piece one can imagine is made by Lefton in the Sweet Violets pattern. 42 items are featured, all numbering in the 2800 range, in Lefton' s 1964 catalog, showing the 12" platter, 3.75" mug and 4.25" ivy pot as discontinued items. Items not discontinued are cake plate, dinner plate, cup and saucer, snack set, canister set, candy box, oil and vinegar set, spice jar, wall pocket, covered cheese dish, pitchers in two different sizes, sugar and creamer, coffee pot, egg cup, two- and three- compartment dishes, gravy boat, divided vegetable dish, candle holders, jam jar, salt and peppers, butter dish, tidbit trays, spoon rest, platters in two sizes, salad bowls, and covered vegetable dish.

SWEETIE

THUMBLINA (Honey Bun)

In Lefton's 1964 catalog this little gal is called "Honey Bun". There are five items pictured, #1690 to #1710, including a jam jar, teapot, sugar and creamer, salt and pepper shakers and cookie jar.

TIFFANY ROSE

TISKET A TASKET

This is a yellow basket weave pattern with vegetables in relief found in Lefton's 1974 catalog. Numbering in the 7000s, there are thirteen items pictured, including a canister set, cookie jar, salt and pepper shakers, pitcher and bowl, creamer and sugar in two sizes, teapot, mug, soup tureen, butter dish, spoon rest, wall pocket, and egg plate.

TO A WILD ROSE

A serving pattern found in Lefton's 1965 catalog, numbering from 2562 to 2603, and including teapot, coffee pot, sugar and creamer, cup and saucer, two-tier tidbit tray, jam jar, pitcher, tumble up, snack sets, cake plate, plates, bone dishes, three sizes of nappy dishes, salt and pepper shakers, and three shapes of candy dishes.

TRIPLEX

Christmas Crystal seen in Lefton's 1974-75 Holiday catalog, numbering from 183-206. Items include vases, bell, ice bucket, compote, candy box, cordial set and candle holders. This pattern is all white with large red and green holly berries and leaves, and gold trim.

VICTORIAN

Figurines of men, women and children of that time period.

VINEYARD

Of the sixteen items shown in Lefton's 1964 catalog, all numbering in the 7000s,

many were discontinued such as the 9.25" plates, cookie jar, compote, mug and pitcher. Not discontinued includes sugar and creamer, coffee pot, cup and saucer, two- and three-compartment dishes, jam jar, relish dish, salt and pepper shakers, candy box, two-tier tidbit tray, and candleholders.

VIOLET CHINTZ

VIOLET HEIRLOOM

VIOLETTE

Numbering in the 03000s, this decorative pattern is pictured in Lefton's 1986 catalog, and consists of picture frames, vases, pitcher and bowls, trinket boxes, bells, ring holders, and baskets.

WHITE CLASSIC

WHITE HOLLY

Lefton's 1974-75 Holiday catalog shows a wide variety of this pattern, numbering from 6048 to 6075. Items include planters, plates, candleholders, bell, two-, three-, and four-compartment dishes, salt and pepper shakers, covered candy boxes, mug, basket, pitcher with bowl, cookie jar, trays, teapot, cream and sugar, and two sizes of sleighs.

WOODLAND

These are miniatures animals consisting of raccoons, mice, owls, bunnies, frogs, squirrels, and chipmunks, and came in three different poses to a set. Seen in Lefton' s 1974-75 Holiday catalog.

YELLOW BIRD

This series is found in the 1974-75 Lefton Holiday catalog, showing a four-piece canister set, cookie jar, and soup tureen, #289 to #310.

YELLOW TULIP

Canister set, tureen, butter dish, mug, compote and spoon rest, among other pieces of this Yellow Tulip are found in Lefton's 1974 catalog, #6700s to 7100s.

YULETIDE HOLLYBERRY

Pictured in Lefton's 1974-75 Holiday book, this pattern is very similar to the English Hollyberry with the exception of more red berries and green leaves and heavier gold trim, and this pattern is apparently not bone china. Catalog shows a teapot #7805, plate #7802, lemon dish #7821, pitcher with bowl #7811, and a cream and sugar #7803.

Pricing

Pricing, I believe, is the most difficult task of any author, for any book about collecting. Many hours of research has been done on pricing, using for a basis a combination of estate auctions, antique shops, flea markets, private collectors, and dealers. Internet auctions have been considered also, although the prices on these auctions are so flexible, it's quite unbelievable. I have seen a Rose Chintz egg cup go for over $200, and a lovely head vase booked at $100 go for $20, so it's quite difficult to base prices from those auctions for this book as they are not realistic. I've tried to find a "happy medium" for pricing using all of the above avenues. Some of you will think the pricing in this book is too high while others will think it's too low.

Who really determines pricing and actual worth? As a buyer and/or a seller, you do. I both buy and sell and have to make these decisions often. There are times when I don't buy something I really want because I feel the price is way out of line. At other times I won't sell a piece lower because I feel the price is reasonable and fair. The bottom line on pricing is that you as the buyer or the seller must make that decision no matter what a "book price" may be.

Many of the Lefton items are very fragile, making it somewhat difficult to find pieces in mint condition. Yet these mint pieces are still to be found if one looks long enough. Some of my best buys have been from dingy flea markets and antique store basements where everything has sat and gathered dust for a long time.

Please keep in mind that my intent is not to set prices for Lefton China! The prices found in this book are to be used as a guideline and not as gospel; they are retail prices and for items in mint condition. Expect the price to be much lower for damaged items and unless you want the piece to complete a collection or it is extremely rare, I'd really think twice before buying it unless the pricing is very reasonable. A damaged piece is usually of little value to the collector or the dealer for resale.

Americana (Rose)

Americana Rose is one of the very loveliest and most sought-after pattern in the Lefton line. The color and detail on this pattern is so exquisite and colorful. 44 of these pieces are found in an undated Lefton catalog from the 1950s, numbering from 939 to 980. In this catalog they are called "Pink Rose Line". 56 of them are found in Lefton's 1964 catalog and most of the pieces are in the 900 numbers. Stickers found on this pattern were used from 1953-71. In the 1964 catalog, the match box, salt box, compote, candle holder, console bowl, egg cup, gravy boat, spoon rest with salt shaker, and the 10.5" plate were shown as discontinued. Items in this Americana pattern that were imported to Canada that I found are numbered in the 6000/7000 range.

Salt and pepper shakers, 4", #955. $25-30.

Bottom mark on salt and peppers.

Compote, 8" round and 3" high, #940. $70-75.

Celery dish, 12" long, #160. $35-40.

Two-compartment dish, 10" long, #938. $65-70.

One-tier tidbit tray, 9.5" round, #943. $60-65.

Jam Jar, 4.5", #6973. For some reason, there are two tiny holes drilled out on either side of the little rose on the top. I have another one that is not from Canada that does not have these holes. They are from the factory, so I'm guessing that they were an error. $45-50.

Covered casserole dish, 9" round and 5" high, #978. $110-120.

Bottom marks on jam jar #6973. This piece was made for Canada, and has the ESD stamp and number.

Spoon rest and shaker. 4" shaker and 7" spoon rest. #961. I've had several collectors ask me if this is an egg holder and not a spoon rest. In Lefton's catalog, it is called a spoon rest; I just wanted to clarify that. $130-140.

Two-tier tidbit tray, 8.5" high, #942. $95-100.

One-tier tidbit tray, 7.5" round, #941. $45-50.

Bottom marks on canister set #946.

Four-piece canister set ranging in size from 8.5" down to 5", #946. $215-220.

This piece is very unique. It isn't the cookie jar, unless they produced two kinds, as the cookie jar is shorter and has two handles on the sides. It does have the same number as the cookie jar, #943, but I have not found it in any of the catalogs I have researched. This piece measures 10". $65-70.

Egg cup, 3.5", #960. $40-45.

Cup and saucer, #957 and #963. $40-45.

Match safe/holder, hangs on wall, 6.5", #968. $100-110.

Salt box, hangs on wall, 5" with a wood top, #969. $125-135. *Courtesy of Janis Cromer.*

Angels

Angel Bride, white porcelain with applied pink roses and spaghetti trim, 3.5". #KW8273. Stamp used 1946–50. $50-55.

Matte finish angel trinket box for April, 4". #3447, $28-33.

Bottom marks on angel trinket box. Stamp used 1950 to at least 1970. Sticker used 1953–71.

Back view of angel Bride. She has gold wings and intricate gold trim.

Boy angel playing violin, matte finish, 3.5". #KW766. (This number was also used on a musical boy and girl, 4"). $20-25. Sticker used 1953-71.

February boy angel, white bisque with gold trim and red heart, 4.5". #1952. $25-30.

Bottom marks for February boy angel. Sticker used 1946-53.

Pair of porcelain angel candle climbers, 3". #1315. $30-35 pair.

Bottom markings for angel candle climbers. Sticker used 1953-71.

White porcelain angel with gold and spaghetti trim, holding a candle, 6.5". #221. Stamp used 1946-50. $60-65.

Precious baby angel on green leaf plaque in porcelain, with applied birds and pink roses, 3" long. #K8145. This one was found in an undated Lefton catalog from the 1950s. At that time they sold for $6.00 per dozen in two poses. Stamp used 1946-50. $50-55.

Angel child with woodland animals, porcelain. This one is with a squirrel. 2" high, #8146. These were found in an undated Lefton catalog, from the 1950s. There were three poses; they sold for $4.80 per dozen. $50-55.

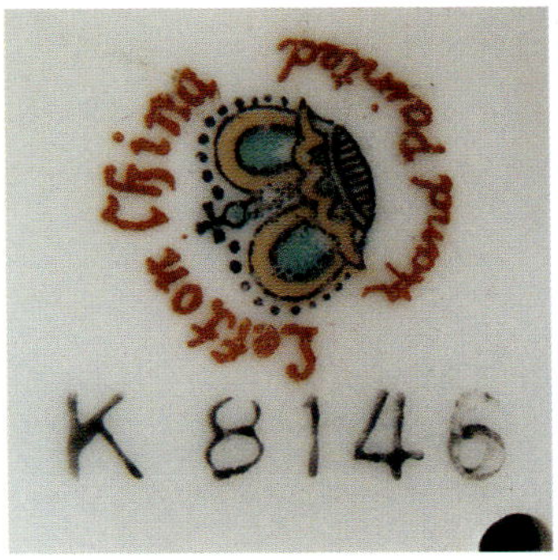

Bottom marks on angel with squirrel. Stamp used 1946-50.

Madonna with baby and two side angels, blue and white, 4" and 2.5". #3904. Sticker used 1953-71. $55-60.

Bisque angel bust, 4", # KW1415N. This one is part of a set. $80-85 for set of two.

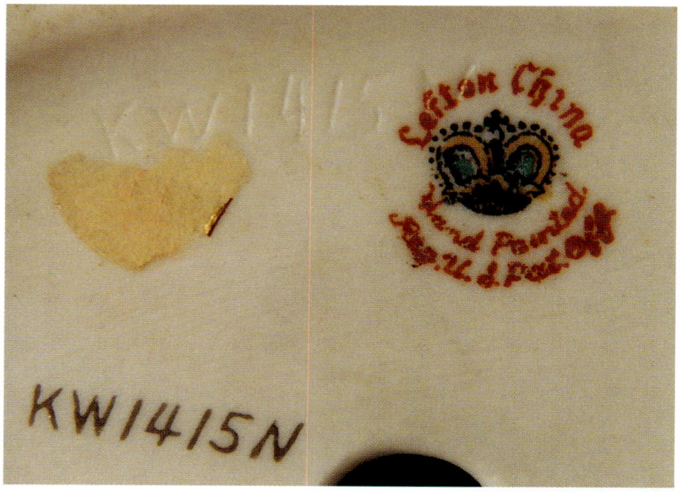

Bottom marks for angel bust. Stamp used 1949-64.

Bottom marks for angel with candle holder. Sticker used 1953-71.

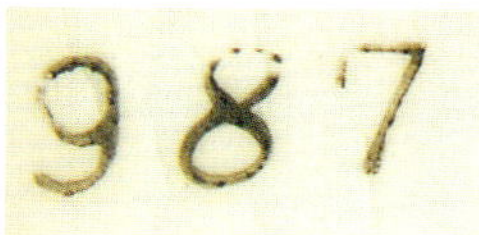

White porcelain angel beside bird bath candle holder with applied birds, gold trim and applied pink roses. 5" high and 6" across base, #987. $50-55. *Courtesy of Heather Roswell.*

Pair of boy angel candle huggers, white porcelain with gold trim and lace cloth wings, 2.5". No number. Sticker used 1946-53. $30-35 pair.

Porcelain angel in blue gown with gold trim, 4.5", #KW002. Stamp used 1949-64. Sticker used 1946-53. $40-45.

White porcelain angel playing a horn with pink applied flowers, spaghetti hair and gold trim. 4", #K8192. $40-45.

Porcelain boy angel with harp, 5", #614. Sticker used 1960-83. $40-45.

Bottom markings on angel with horn. Stamp used 1946-50. Sticker used 1946-53.

Angel in peach colored dress playing horn with applied flowers on head, 3.5", #149. Sticker used 1946-53. $25-30.

Angel Series #3332

This monthly angel series was and still is extremely popular. These angels are listed in Lefton catalogs 1964, 1965, 1967-68 and 1973-74. Produced in white porcelain bisque, 4" high, with gold trim and halos, they are all holding baskets of flowers. Except for May, June, July and November, they all have an applied flower on the skirts. These could have possibly come from different factories; I have also found three different stickers on these, which are seen on the bottom marks. By comparing these stickers and their dates, we can see that these angels were made sometime between 1962 and 1971. Price range is $45-50.

February. Sticker used 1960-83.

January. Sticker used 1953-71.

March. Sticker used 1960-83.

April.

June. Sticker used 1960-83. *Courtesy of Stephenie Goodsite.*

Bottom mark on April. Sticker used 1953-71.

July. (no sticker)

Bottom marks on July.

May. Sticker used 1953-71

August. Sticker used 1953-71.

September. Sticker used 1960-83.

October. Sticker used 1953-71.

November.

Bottom marks for November. Sticker used 1962-90.

December.

Bottom marks for December. Sticker used 1960-83.

Angel Series #489

Monthly angel series #489 are all 4" high and porcelain. They have the month written across the front of their skirts, applied birth stones, flowers, halos, gold tipped wings and spaghetti trim. Each facial detail is different; some have pony tails, pig tails, curly hair or straight hair. These angels were found in the following Lefton catalogs: undated 1958-61, 1964, and 1967-68. Price range is $50-60.

January, "Snowdrop Garnet".

February, "Violet Amethyst".

March, "Daffodil Aquamarine".

April, "Daisy Diamond".

May, "Carnation Emerald".

Stamp, sticker and number found on all #489 angels. Stamp used 1950 to at least 1970. Sticker used 1953-71.

July, "Water Lily Ruby".

June, "Rose Pearl"

August, "Poppy Peridot".

September, "Morning Glory Sapphire".

November, "Mums Topaz". *Courtesy of Nicole Osborn.*

October, "Cosmos Rose Zircon". (Please excuse her broken halo, she had an accident.)

December, "Poinsettia Blue Zircon".

Angel Series #6224

Monthly angel series #6224 are 4.5" high and porcelain. They all have the month written on the front of their dresses, applied birth stones and flowers, no halos, and gold tipped wings. Each of them is wearing a ribbon or hair band in their hair and their hair is in different styles. These angels are found in the Lefton catalog dated 1973-74. Price range is $45-50.

Bottom markings on the angels of this series. Sticker used 1962-90. Numbers used with this sticker are small and bold.

Bottom markings on some of the angels of this series. Sticker used 1960-83. Interesting that this series has two different stickers. Perhaps they came from different factories. Numbers are larger and plain with these stickers.

January, Garnet.

February, Amethyst.

March, light Emerald.

April, Diamond.

May, dark Emerald.

June, Pearl.

July, Ruby.

August, Peridot.

September, Sapphire.

October, Rose Zircon.

November, Topaz. *Courtesy of Jessica Tyson.*

December, Blue Zircon.

Porcelain angel holding candle. This one was not given a name. Gold halo and wings, applied pink flowers and spaghetti trim. 3.5", #808-C. Small black oval Made in Japan sticker. Stamp used 1946-50. $60-65

This little angel looks to have had a gold paint job. I'm not sure that the gold paint is original. 3.5", #808 with no name. Stamp used 1946-50. Small black oval Made in Japan sticker. $60-65

This little angel is almost identical to #808 except she is wearing no halo. 3.5", #808-C. Also, she has the Made In Occupied Japan stamp on the bottom instead of the Lefton stamp. $65-70

Porcelain angel holding what looks to be a rag in one hand and a gold star in the other hand. There are gold stars and spaghetti trim at the bottom of her skirt and pink applied flowers at the base. She has a gold halo. 3.5", #808. Stamp used 1946-50. $65-70

Bottom markings on angel #808-C. This stamp was used from 1945-53.

Animals and Birds

Bottom marks for humming bird. Sticker used 1962-90. Stamp used 1955-present.

Tan and white porcelain colt with dark brown eyes and ears, matte finish, 5" long, #80520. $40-45.

Bottom marks for colt. Sticker used 1953-71.

Matte finish Humming bird on wood base, 3.5" (without wood base). #KW464. $38-43.

Three little white porcelain kittens with yellow applied flowers, 3.5" and 4", #H4845. Sticker used 1953-71. $28-32 for set of three.

Large white Persian cat, 9", #H2203. $40-45. *Courtesy of Stuart Brown.*

Black bisque bear, 5", #KW4912. $45-50.

Bottom marks on black bear, stamp used 1950-55, #KW4912.

Koala Bear with cub on her back, 6", #KW4751. $50-55.

Bottom marks on Koala Bear. Stamp used 1955-present.

Pink porcelain deer with gold trim, rhinestone eyes and spaghetti fur trim, 5" high. Stamp used 1946-53. $40-45.

Black and white bisque rooster, 5.5". #KW1051A. Stamp used 1955-present. Sticker used 1953-71. $35-40.

Pair of bears in chef hats, 3" high. #H174. Sticker used 1962-80. $12-15 pair.

Pink porcelain cat with gold bow, rhinestone eyes and spaghetti fur trim. 5" high. Sticker used 1946-53. $40-45.

White porcelain hound dog, 6" long. #80521. Sticker used 1946-53. $50-55.

Bottom marks for House Finch. Stamp used 1955-present. Sticker used 1953-1971.

House Finch, matte finish, 5", #KW4206. $40-45.

Pair of doves on tree branch, hand painted white bisque, 2.5", #734. Sticker used 1962-90. $15-18.

Bottom marks on Flycatcher. Stamp used 1955-present.

Bisque bird, Flycatcher, 5", #KW1184. $35-40.

Banks

Black and white porcelain skunk—For My New Fur. 7", #H3621. Sticker used 1953-71. $20-25.

Porcelain Uncle Sam in red, white, blue and gold—For My Income Tax. 7" high, #882. Sticker used 1953-71. $35-40.

Bottom mark for France bank. Sticker used 1953-71.

Round bank with a scene from France and *Pour Les Vacences* written on the top. 6.5" high, #2276. $20-25.

Porcelain Elf—Barrel O'Money, 9" high. This is a Marika's Original by Lefton©. Found in Lefton' s 1974-75 Holiday Catalog. $60-65. *Courtesy of Robin Goodsite.*

Gold color clock, porcelain with daisies, 6.5" high. #H6145. Sticker used 1960-83. $20-23.

Black, gray and white porcelain Scottie. These were produced in at least two sizes, 4.5" and 5.5", #H1240. $20-25 and $30-35.

Large 9" porcelain Grandma bank—For Grandma's Pride and Joy. #5719. Sticker used 1953-71. $35-40.

Bottom marks for Scottie bank. Sticker used 1962-90.

Bells

White porcelain Valentine girl with red hearts, gold bow and spaghetti type trim, 4.5", #8335. Sticker used 1946-53. $30-35.

White porcelain girl with gold accents, applied pink flowers and spaghetti type trim. 3", #6214. Sticker used 1946-53. $28-32.

Pink porcelain bell with applied pink roses, green leaves and gold spaghetti trim. 2.5" high, #8700. Stamp used 1946-50. $25-30.

Large Fantasia pattern, 5", Sticker used 1960-83. $18-22.

Bloomer girl, matte finish, holding dress out at sides, 4". #8276. Sticker used 1960-83. Not shown in catalogs researched. $30-35.

This little bloomer girl has applied lace around the bottom of her dress and she's holding a package. 4", #1216. Stamp used 1955-present. Not shown in catalogs researched. $40-45.

Back of bloomer girl #KW1702.

Matte bloomer in blue with applied flowers, 3.5", #KW1702. $45-50.

Bottom markings on #KW1702.

Bisque bloomer in pink ruffled dress holding yellow bird, 4.5", #KW3757. Not shown in catalogs researched. $40-45.

Bisque bloomer in blue ruffled dress holding yellow bird, laying down. 4.5" long, #KW3757. Not shown in catalogs researched. $40-45.

Bottom markings on both girls #3757. Sticker used 1962-90. Stamp used 1955-present.

Bloomer in bisque with blue dress and pony tail, 4" long, #8418. Stamp used 1955-present. Sticker used 1960-83. Not found in catalogs researched. $25-30.

Bisque bloomer in blue holding her hat with dress up and bloomers showing in the back, 4.5", #KW3701. $45-50.

Back view of blue gal #KW3701.

Another style of bloomer #KW3701, holding hat with both hands, and bloomers showing in front. $45-50.

Pink bloomer holding hat with bloomers showing in back, 4.5", #KW3701. $45-50.

Another pose of pink bloomer holding hat in both hands and bloomers showing in front, #KW3701. $45-50.

Bottom markings on all girls #KW3701. Gold stamped number. Sticker used 1946-53.

Candle Holders

White porcelain candle holders with applied Dogwood flowers and gold sponge trim, 3" high, #357. Sticker used 1946-53. $60-65 a pair.

Bunny Girls in white porcelain with gold trim, 3.5", #346. Sticker used 1946-53. $45-50 pair. *Courtesy of Jan Matthews.*

Pink porcelain candle holders with pink and blue Forget Me Not flowers and gold trim, 3". Stamp used 1946-53. $50-55 a pair.

White bisque candle holders with pink, blue and yellow applied flowers and gold trim. 5" across, #KW3211. $60-65

Bottom marks for #285 candle holders. Stamp used 1946-50.

Cornucopia-shaped candle holders, pink porcelain with Lily of the Valley flowers and gold sponge trim, 3.5". #285. $50-55 a pair.

Paper sticker, gold and red in the shape of a bee with "Bee Line" in black.

White glossy porcelain with tulip-type holders and brown handles from the "Bee Line" collection. There is a small applied bee to all pieces in this pattern. 6" across and 2" high, #1593. $45-50.

Country Squire candle holder, 6" round, #1613. $25-30.

Bottom markings on Country Squire candle holder. Sticker used 1946-53.

Canister Sets and Cookie Jars

Three-piece white porcelain basket weave with "Dancing Leaves", 6", 7", and 8", #7277. Sticker used 1960-83. $100-125, 4-piece set.

Chili Peppers, two-piece, green porcelain, 9", and 6.5", #5948. $125-140, 4-piece set.

Bottom marks on Chili Peppers canister. Sticker used 1960-1983.

Four-piece white and yellow porcelain canister, 10", 8.5.", 7" and 5.5", #1698. $110-135, 4-piece set.

Three-piece brown "Sack O" canister set with burlap texture. 7", 6", 5" and 4", #0484. $80-90.

Bottom marks on canister #1698. Sticker used 1962-90.

Chili Pepper cookie jar, 10", #5949. $75-85.

Cookie jar with white speckled background, blue bird and flowers, 10", #4856. $60-65.

Bottom marks for cookie jar #4856. Sticker used 1953-71.

This cookie jar appears to go with the "Sack O" canisters, but there is nothing written on the front of it. Perhaps an error from the factory? 9", #0484. $45-50.

Bottom mark for cookie jar #0484. Sticker used 1960-83.

White and yellow porcelain cookie jar with spring flowers, 12", #1698. Sticker used 1962-90. $40-45.

Dancing Leaves cookie jar, 10", #7277. $55-60.

Bottom marks for cookie jar #7277. Sticker used 1960-83.

Large, heavy cookie jar with white weave background and hand painted fruit, 12.5", no number. $50-55

Four-piece canister set, large with white weave back ground and hand painted fruit. Sizes range from 8" to 11.5", no number. $85-90, four-piece set.

Bottom sticker on both the four-piece canister and the cookie jar. No information found for dates of sticker used. This is the only sticker I have personally seen from Mexico, possibly used from 1970 to present.

Four-piece mushroom canister set, sizes ranging from 5" to 8", #H6561. Sticker used 1960-83. $80-85, four-piece set.

Christmas

Four-porcelain angels sitting on a candy cane sleigh (this is one piece), 10" long and 3" high, #626. $55-60.

Bottom markings on candy cane sleigh. Sticker used 1953-71. Stamp used 1950 to at least 1970.

Colorful Mr. and Mrs. Santa banks for Christmas Fund, porcelain, 6", #2114. Sticker used 1962-90. $45-50 pair.

White deer salt and pepper shakers, 3.5", #1669. Sticker used 1962-90. $8-10.

Three Christmas girl bells with spaghetti trim, 4". No number. Sticker used 1946-53. Stamp used 1950 to at least 1970. $40-45 each.

Votive candle holder girl angel, porcelain, 4", no number. Sticker used 1960-83. Shown in the 1974-75 Lefton catalog, came with candle. $12-15.

Rudolph child's handled cup and bowl. Cup is 3.5" high, bowl is 6" round. #4371. This is a rather rare set. $130-140, two-piece set.

Bottom markings on Rudolph bowl. Sticker used 1953-71.

Rudolph salt and pepper shakers, 3", #4370. Sticker used 1953-71. $40-45.

Porcelain angel nodder, 5", #4801. The top removes from the base. Unusual piece. Sticker used 1953-71. $75-80.

Santa-type Elf wall plaque carrying bag over shoulder and holding lamp, 6.5", #4078. Sticker used 1953-71. $35-40.

Porcelain boy angel, 4.5", no number. Sticker used 1946-53. $40-45. *Courtesy of Stuart Brown.*

Porcelain girl angel, 4.5", no number. Sticker used 1946-53. $40-45. *Courtesy of Stuart Brown.*

Pair of girl Christmas angels, 4.5", no number. Sticker used 1946-53. $35-40 each. *Courtesy of Stuart Brown.*

Candy cane girls with red bows, 3.25" and 4.75", no number. Stickers used 1946-53. $20-23 and $25-28. *Courtesy of Linda and Jim Batt.*

Christmas tree boot ornament, porcelain, 4". There is also a small hole in the back for hanging on a wall. Sticker used 1953-71. No number. $12-15.

Sweet little angel bells, porcelain with holly on front of dresses. Four-piece set spelling out "Noel". 3.5", #80283. Stamp used 1950 to at least 1970. Date on these is 1956. $55-60 for set of four. *Courtesy of Linda and Jim Batt.*

Little bare boy figurines with holly leaves, 3.5", no number. Sticker used 1960-83. $35-40 each.

Rear view of little bare boys.

Candle salt and peppers, 3", #1556. Sticker used 1943-71. $20-25. *Courtesy of Linda and Jim Batt.*

White porcelain deer candle holder, 3.5" long and 3" high, #707. Sticker used 1953-71. $18-23.

Pair of pink and white Snow Flake kids, 4", #HH80135. $65-70 pair.

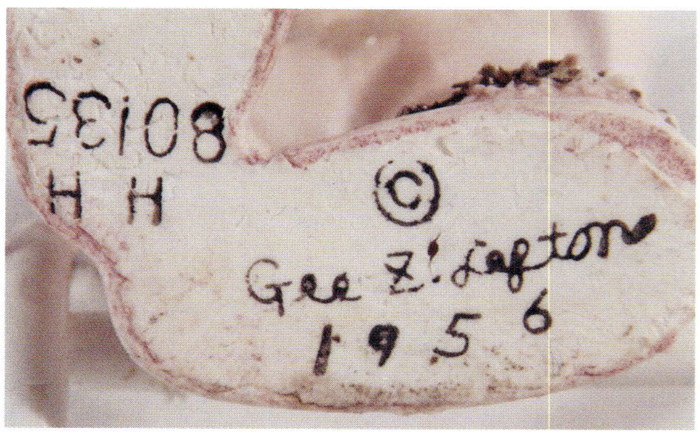

Bottom marks on pink Snow Flake girl. Stamp used 1956 to at least 1970.

Christmas gravy boat with underplate. This looks like the White Holly pattern, but has a smooth surface, unlike the rest of the White Holly in the Lefton catalogs, which all have a raised pattern in the white surface. 8.5" long, #2728. $40-45.

Bottom marks on Christmas gravy boat. Sticker used 1953-71.

Boy and girl Christmas bells, 3.5", #019. Stamp used 1950 to at least 1970. $30-35 pair. *Courtesy of Linda and Jim Batt.*

Coffee, Tea, Cream and Sugar

Unusual porcelain coffee pot with black background and beautiful, large pink roses. This pattern is similar to the Midnight Rose pattern. 8.5", #23284, Canadian ESD. $85-90.

Vineyard 9" coffee pot, #3028. Sticker used 1953-71. $70-75.

Vineyard sugar and cream set, 4" and 5". #3029. Sticker used 1953-71. $25-30.

Black cream and sugar with large pink roses, 3.75" and 4.25". #23284. Canadian ESD. $45-50.

Bottom marks for #23284. I have been unable to find much information on these stamps from Canada, sorry to say, as far as dating goes.

Brown Heritage fruit coffee pot, 8.5", #20591. Stamp used 1955-present. Sticker used 1953-71. $135-145. *Courtesy of Stuart Brown.*

Brown Heritage fruit cream and sugar set, 4", #20592. $60-65. Stamp used 1955-present. Sticker used 1953-71. *Courtesy of Stuart Brown.*

Country Squire sugar and creamer, 3.5", #1607. $40-45.

Bottom marks for Country Squire set. Sticker used 1953-71.

Country Squire Tea/Coffee Pot. White porcelain with rooster and green trim, 7", #1606. $75-80.

Expresso Wisteria coffee pot, 10.75", #3159. $90-95. *Courtesy of Stuart Brown.*

Expresso Wisteria cream and sugar, 4", #3162. $35-40. *Courtesy of Stuart Brown*

Tangerine Expresso coffee pot, 10.75", #3156. Stamp used 1955-present. Sticker used 1953-71. $90-95. *Courtesy of Stuart Brown.*

Brown Heritage floral two-cup teapot, 4", #476. Stamp used 1949-64. Shown in Lefton's 1964 catalog and sold for $9.00 per dozen, wholesale. $95-100. *Courtesy of Stuart Brown.*

Oval Moss Rose cream and sugar with gold trim, 3.5", #6842. $55-60.

Bottom marks for #6842. Stamp used 1955-present.

Bottom markings on blue rose tea bag holder. Stamp used 1955-present.

Tea bag holder, blue rose chintz type on white porcelain with silver trim, 4.5" across, #6672. $25-30.

Tea bag holder, flower cup with handle. 1.5" high and 3.5" round, #2516. Sticker used 1953-71. $20-25.

Bottom marks on tomato teapot. Sticker used 1953-71.

Four-cup red and green tomato teapot, 5", #3149. $75-80.

Covered Dishes/Boxes

Bottom marks on cheese dish #3924. Sticker used 1953-71.

Dutch Blue pattern covered cheese dish found in Lefton's 1967-68 catalog. 3.5" high and 8" across base, #3924. $45-55.

Bottom marks for #KA678. Stamp used 1953-75. Sticker used 1953-71.

Powder dish, white footed porcelain with roses, 5". This dish was produced in two sizes. There is also a 3", #KA678. 5" $40-45, and 3" $30-35.

Beautiful swan candy dish with lid, #R2091. I found this lovely item in an old Lefton brochure. It says that these swan dishes were produced in 1954, only 900 of them. I would consider this a rather rare item. Measures 7" long and 4" high. $150-160.

Candy dish with applied fruit, 6". There are several pieces of this pattern, such as vases, planters and dishes. They were produced in 1956. $40-45. *Courtesy of Stuart Brown.*

Rose Chintz instant coffee jar with corked lid, 5.5". Found in an undated Lefton catalog from the 1950s. #890R. $50-55. *Courtesy of Stuart Brown*.

Lady Bug trinket box, white bisque, 4" long, #658. Stamp used 1955-present. Sticker used 1960-83. $12-15.

Bottom marks for #KW642. I believe this stamp started in 1977 and is still in use.

Small matte October trinket or ring box, 2.4" , #KW642. $10-12.

White Gold Leaf pattern three-footed pin box with gold roses hand painted on lid, 2.5", #3375. Stamp used 1955-present. Sticker used 1953-71. $15-20

Bottom marks on Gold Leaf pin box. Stamp used 1955-present. Sticker used 1953-71.

Burlap look honey pot with one handle, 5", #H1672. $18-23.

Bottom marks on honey pot. Sticker used 1962-90.

Brown porcelain covered cheese container, 4", #H1419. $20-25.

Bottom markings on cheese container. Sticker used 1962-90.

Decorative Items

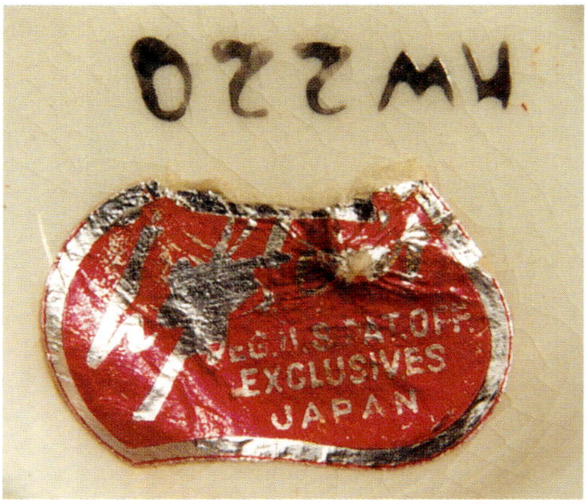

Bottom markings for egg cup #KW220. Sticker used 1953-71.

Winking figural egg cup with removable top, 4", #KW220. $40-55.

Pear N Apple oil lamp, 11", #4336. Sticker used 1960-83. $75-80.

White porcelain flower frog with three removable cherubs, each of them able to hold a small candle. 8" round, #1097. Unusual piece. $125-135.

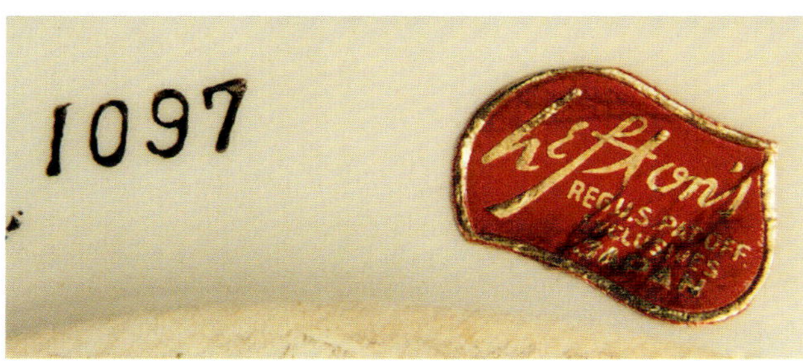

Bottom marks for flower frog #1097. Sticker used 1953-71.

Figural Russian Dressing bottle, 9.5", #2090. Sticker used 1953-71. $55-60.

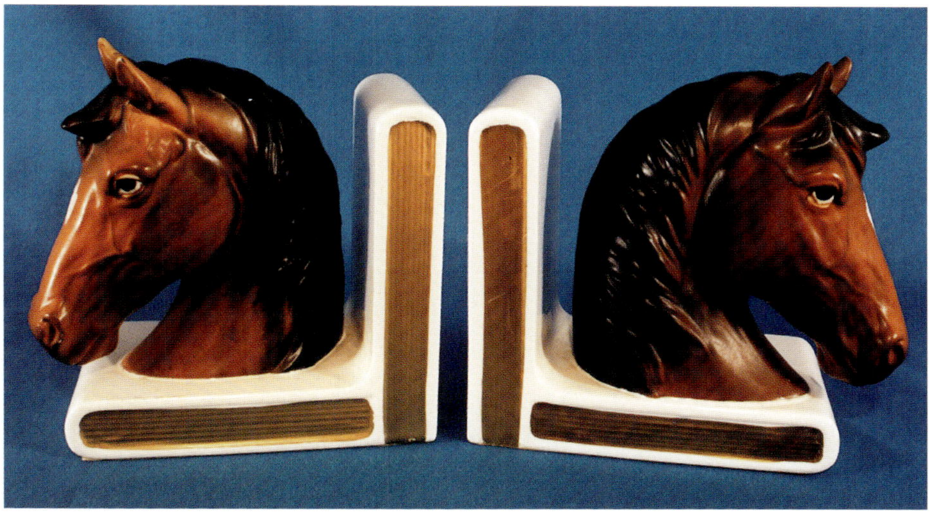

Brown horse head bookends, 5" high, #H1681. $60-65.

Bottom marks for horse head bookends. Sticker used 1960-83.

Double picture frame, white porcelain, matte finish with applied flowers, 6" by 4". #KW4997. Sticker used 1960-83. $40-45.

Mr. Toodles napkin holder, 5", no number. Sticker used 1953-71. $50-55.

Dutch girl egg cup, porcelain, 3", #2700. Sticker used 1953-71. $40-45.

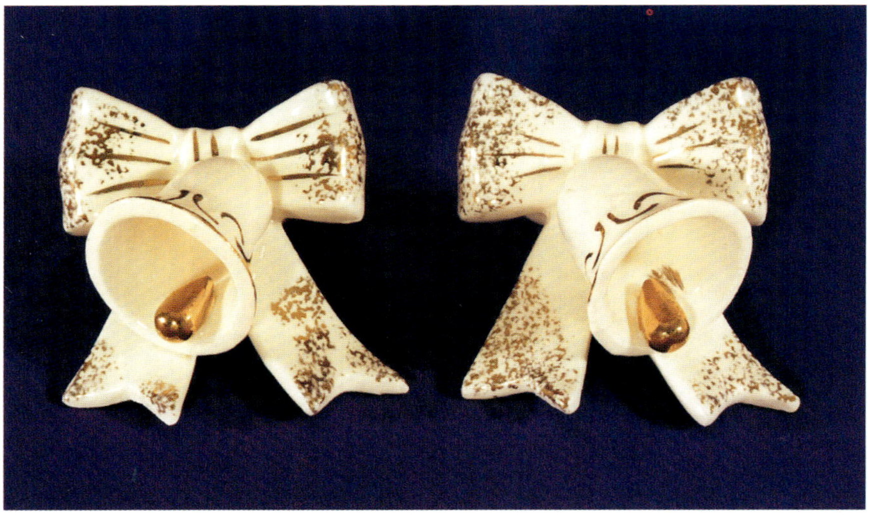

Pair of wedding bell candle climbers (or could be used for napkin holders), white porcelain with gold sponge trim. These came six to a box. 2.5" high, #992. $25-30 pair.

Bottom markings for candle climbers. Sticker used 1946-53.

Bottom marks for Tumble Up. Stamp used 1955-present.

Tumble Up with Forget Me Not flowers and gold trim, 7", #SL4188. $65-70.

Bottom mark for high heeled shoe. This is an unusual stamp. Very seldom seen. Probably used in the late '40s or early '50s.

Pink porcelain high-heeled shoe with beautiful applied white lace and gold trim, pink roses and blue Forget Me Not flowers. 4" high. $35-40.

Four-piece condiment set with roses. Has tiny porcelain spoon. 4.5", #039. Sticker used 1946-53. $40-45.

Kewpie night light, 6.5", #5718. Sticker used 1962-90. $45-50.

Lovely white glass lamp with hand painted flowers and gold trim, 8" . Has round black stamp on the bottom. (See chapter on Markings).

Pekingese book ends, 5". Sticker used 1953-71. $75-80.

Porcelain light switch plate with hand painted violets, 5", #197. $20-25.

Bottom markings on light switch. Sticker used 1953-71.

Four-piece white porcelain centerpiece with "exquisitely detailed porcelain flowers", 8" round when put together. Shown in an undated Lefton catalog from the 1950s, #8078. Catalog says this piece came in either pink or white. Stamp used 1946-50. $90-95

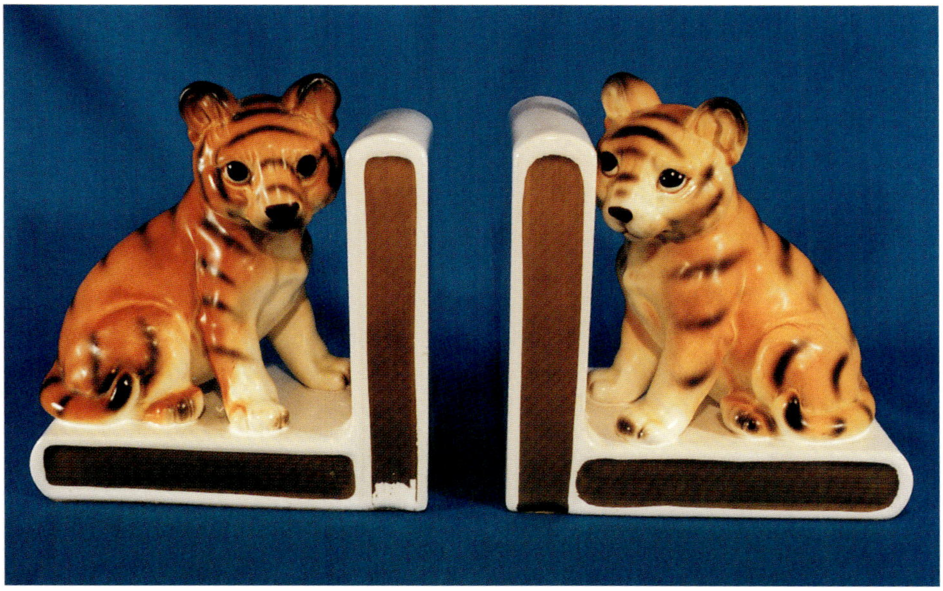

Tiger cub bookends, 5.5" high, no number. Sticker used 1960-83. $40-45. *Courtesy of Kathleen Osborn.*

Dishes, Tidbits and Compotes

Two-tier tidbit, To A Wild Rose, 9" high, #NE2592. $70-80.

Bottom marks for two-tier tidbit tray, #NE2592. Stamp used 1955-present.

Tidbit tray, To A Wild Rose, 6.5" round, #NE2593. $35-40.

Tidbit tray, To A Wild Rose, 9.5" round, #NE2594. $40-45.

Applied fruit compote, #2603. This was made in at least two sizes, 7" and 8". Produced in 1956, this pattern also comes in vases, planters and candy dishes. $65-70. *Courtesy of Stuart Brown*.

Eastern Elegance dish, pink with gold sponge trim and feathers, 5" long, #KW2957. $45-50.

Della Robbia compote, 8.5" round, #2086. Sticker used 1953-71. $40-45.

Bottom marks for dish #KW2957. Double stamped. Multi colored stamp was used from 1946-50. Black stamp was used 1950 to at least 1970.

Bottom marks for plate #105. Stamp used 1949-64. Sticker used 1953-71.

Heavenly Rose plate with handle, 9", #105. $50-55.

Early American Rooster dish. I am not sure if this is an ashtray, spoon rest or candy dish. 5.5", #001. $20-25. *Courtesy of Stuart Brown*

Two-compartment dish, Bee Line, 8". #1588. $45-50.

Brown Heritage floral candy dish, 6.5" long. #4670. $30-35.

Bottom marks for #4670. Stamp used 1955-present.

Double bonbon dish with bird, #CY209. $30-35. *Courtesy of Stuart Brown.*

Bottom marks on swan dish. Stamp used 1968-unknown.

Pink porcelain swan dish with applied flowers and leaves, gold trim, 4", #1398. $30-35.

This lovely swan dish was produced in at least two sizes, 3" and 5.5", and in two colors, pink and white with applied pink and white Forget Me Not flowers and gold trim. #KW8279. (At least, I think the last number is a 9). $40-45 for 3", $55-60 for 5.5".

Bottom markings on swan dish. Stamp used 1946-50.

Dresser Sets and Perfumes

Three-piece white porcelain dresser set with applied flowers, leaves and rhinestones. Powder box is 3.5" and both perfumes are 5.5". This set came in pink or white, #RV90542, and are found in the 1980 Lefton Collector's Guide. There were 4788 produced in each color from 1955-57. Original retail price at that time was $2.00 per set. Now, $100-110 per three-piece set. (Please see Chapter on Identifying Marks.)

Bisque perfume bottle with applied pink roses and light green leaves, 5.5", #842. $40-45.

Pair of light blue lotion bottles, matte finish with hand painted Forget Me Not flowers and gold trim. 5", #8185. $25-30 pair.

Bottom marks on perfume bottle. Stamp used 1949-64. Sticker used 1953-71.

Bottom stamp on blue lotion bottles. Stamp used 1955-present.

Bottom marks on Golden Laurel jars. Stamp used 1955-present.

White Golden Laurel covered jars with gold trim, 7", #2407. $20-25 pair.

Bottom mark on Only A Rose set. Stamp used 1949-64.

Two-piece porcelain perfume bottle set, Only A Rose, 6", #385. This is a front and back view. This set came with a powder box. $100-110 three-piece set.

Pink porcelain perfume set and powder box with applied pink roses, light green leaves and gold sponge trim. Perfumes are 5.5", powder box is 3.5", #9087. Sticker used 1946-53. $110-120, three-piece set. *Courtesy of Stuart Brown.*

Figurines

Girls

Bisque girl with flower baskets in each arm, 5", #KW118B. Stamp used 1955-present. $40-45.

A porcelain Marika's Original girl, 4.5", #4699. Sticker used 1953-71. $40-45.

Set of four colorful Vendor Girls, each with a tray in front of them holding fruit, berries, cheeses and meats. 4.25" high, #H3898. $90-100 set of four.

Bottom marks on all four girls #H3898. Sticker used 1953-71.

Porcelain girl holding white dove, Marika's Original, 5", #458B. Sticker used 1953-71. $35-40.

Porcelain girl nurse with blue dress and white apron, holding chart and looking a little confused. 4.75", #2902. $45-50

Porcelain girl nurse with blue dress and white apron, holding a tray with a milk bottle and cup. 4.75", #TWDO2902. (This one says Made In Taiwan, but has a Japan sticker) I found this interesting as all three of these little nurses came in the same box from the same factory. $45-50.

Porcelain girl nurse with blue dress and white apron. holding a thermometer. 4.75". #2902. $45-50.

Bottom marks on two of the nurses #2902. Sticker used from 1962-90.

Little bisque girl ready for Valentines Day, 3.5", #2733. Stamp used 1955-present. $15-20.

Little miss with bird cage and bird, brown hair, Antique Ivory, 5.5", #KW1004. $45-50. *Courtesy of Jessica Tyson.*

Porcelain girl in yellow, Marika's Original, 6", #4662. $35-40.

Bottom marks for girl #4662. Sticker used 1953-71.

Bottom markings on both Antique Ivory girls. Crown was used 1955-present. Sticker used 1962-90.

Little miss with bird cage and bird, blonde hair, Antique Ivory, 5.5", #KW1004. $45-50.

Two little girls together in one bisque figurine, 4", #2726. Stamp used 1955-present. $20-25.

Two little girls together in one bisque figurine, 4.5", #2726. This must have been a series, but I have not found it in any of the Lefton catalogs I researched. Stamp used 1955-present. $20-25.

Bisque girl feeding duck, 6", #KW5643. $35-40.

Bottom stamp and number on girl feeding duck. Stamp used 1955-present.

Bisque girl holding flowers behind her back with applied flower in her hair, 4.5", #KW843C. These girls were produced in more than one size and pose. On the bottom there is an "N" over "C" and the number. Stamp used 1955-present. $20-25.

Bisque girl in yellow with eyes closed and legs crossed, 4", no number. $20-25.

Mark on bottom of girl in yellow dress. Sticker used 1960-83. Stamp used beginning in 1968. No end date known.

Colonial lady with fan, porcelain with matte finish, 8", #KW7225. $75-80.

Bottom markings for Colonial lady with fan. Stamp used 1955-present.

Bisque lady holding bird and cage, 7.5", #469. Sticker used 1962-90. $60-65.

Bottom markings on lady holding purse. Stamp used 1955-present. Sticker used 1962-90.

Porcelain lady with matte finish, holding purse, 7.5", #KW2623. $45-50.

L'Amour Lady with parasol and purse, pink porcelain with applied lace, spaghetti and gold trim. 6.5", #KW1887. $90-95. *Courtesy of Stuart Brown.*

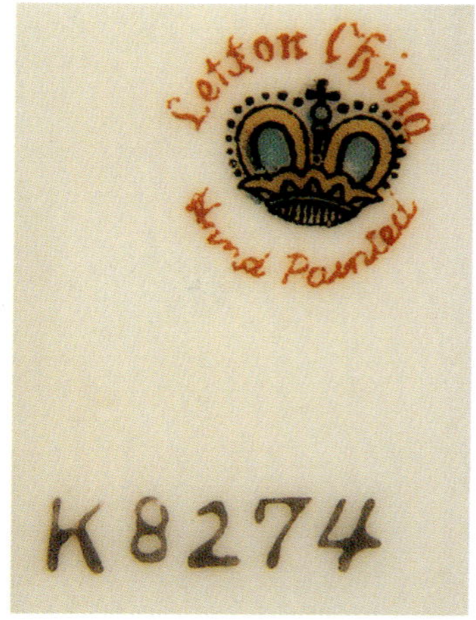

Bottom markings for both ladies #8274. Stamp was used, it seems, from 1946 to at least 1955.

Lovely porcelain lady in white dress with parasol, spaghetti and gold trim, 7.5", #8274. This is a rare piece. $95-100.

Lovely porcelain lady in white dress with spaghetti and gold trim, 7.5", #8274. There were only 1008 of these ladies produced from 1954-55 in pink and white. This information was found in a small booklet by the Lefton China Co. There is no date on it, but it does say , "The year 1980 marked the 40th anniversary of the Geo. Zoltan Lefton Co., producers of fine ceramic giftware". This is a rare piece. $95-100.

Peasant lady in green dress and apron with a scarf on her head, carrying a basket of flowers, 5.5", #2798. Sticker used 1960-83. $50-55.

Porcelain lady in beautiful blue dress and bonnet and holding a parasol. Her name is Corrine and she is 9.5" high, #4230B. Sticker was used 1946-53. $170-180.

Bottom markings for Corrine. Sticker used 1953-71.

Lovely porcelain lady holding a basket of flowers, 6.5". I have two of these. This one is a Canadian import, and is #MR7245. The other one has #418; the sticker was used 1953-71. $75-80.

Bottom marks for lady #MR7245.

Beautiful porcelain lady in white dress and bonnet, with applied pink roses and gold trim, 6.5". You can tell this is an older piece from the 1950s due to the facial features. There is no number on her, but notice the different bottom markings. (Please see chapter on Markings.)

Porcelain Nurse in blue and white, holding a baby, 5.5", #2739. $35-40.

Porcelain Nurse in blue and white, holding a note pad and pen, 5.5", #2739. $35-40.

Porcelain Nurse in blue and white, with a candle, 5.5", #2739. $35-40.

Bottom markings on a three Nurse figurines. Sticker used 1953-71.

Porcelain lady figurine in a dark green dress with applied yellow flowers and gold trim, 7.5". No number. This lady was also produced as a planter. $90-100.

Bottom markings on lady with purse. Stamp used 1950 to at least 1970. Dated 1956.

Porcelain Dutch girl holding buckets, in black dress, white apron and collar, 6". No number. $45-50.

Markings on Dutch lady. Sticker used 1946-53. Stamp used 1946-53.

Lovely Mathilde in yellow dress with applied flowers. On the bottom it says "Mathilde, designed by Marika" and the black ©Lefton stamp. 6", no number. $40-45.

Bottom marks for cowboy. Sticker used 1962-90.

Bisque Cowboy with gun, rope and hat, 9", #XU1477. $60-65.

Continental Cavalry man, bisque, 8.5", #238. Found in Lefton's 1974-75 catalog. Sticker used 1960-83. Stamp used 1955-present. $55-60.

Small bisque boy pushing a cart with a puppy inside. Notice the cute brimmed hat on the puppy. He was found in the 1974-75 Lefton catalog listed under "Andorra" figurines, 6.5". #KW230. $35-40.

Bottom marks on boy with puppy. Stamp used 1955-present. Sticker used 1962-90. *Courtesy of Matthew Roswell.*

Small bisque boy pushing a cart with a puppy inside. There are minor differences in this one compared to the one found in the 1974-75 catalog. Measuring just 6", this one is smaller and the features are a little brighter. #KW00230. $35-40.

Bottom marks on boy with puppy #KW00230. Stamp used 1955-present. Sticker used 1962-90.

Boy with puppy and basket of flowers, bisque, 6.5", #GG5676. Stamp used 1962-present. Sticker used 1962-90. $40-45.

Hand painted matte finish Devil boy, 4", no number. Black stamp used 1950 to at least 1970. $20-25

Grouping of five porcelain red devils. Four of them with spears (the middle one should also have a spear) appear in Lefton's undated 1950s catalog. #113, they came one dozen to a box in four irresistible poses, 2.5". At that time the price was $4.20 per box. The fourth devil here, with the musical instrument, is actually a part of another series called Red Devil musicians. Three poses and priced at $4.20 per dozen, they too are found in the same catalog. $30-35 each.

These four little red devils are sportsmen. Bowler, batter, pitcher and golfer, porcelain, all on white pedestals with gold trim, 3", #K1432. $30-35 each.

Bottom marks on the four red devils. Sticker used 1946-53. Stamp used 1946-50.

Old man and boy, bisque, 8.5", #5241. Sticker used 1960-83. Stamp used 1955-present. $125-130.

Porcelain reclining cowboy, 6", #142. There were three poses of these cowboys found in the undated 1956 Lefton catalog. "Highly colored glaze finish cowboys, in life like poses". They sold at that time for $6.00 per dozen. $40-45 each. *Courtesy of Stuart Brown.*

Porcelain sitting cowboy, 6", #142. $40-45. *Courtesy of Stuart Brown.*

Bottom markings on the Professor. Stamp, used 1950 to at least 1970. This is an example of the little red oval Japan stamp. (See chapter on Markings)

Hand painted bisque gentleman called the Professor, 8", #GG5682NP. $60-65.

Bottom markings on boy by apple tree. Stamp used 1955 to present. (Still doing research on the N over C stamp).

Bisque boy by apple tree, holding an apple, 4.5", #KW3082A. $30-35.

The All-American Politician, 8", #KW7334. $55-60.

Bottom marks on Politician. Stamp used 1955-present.

Boy Series #2300

These little boys of the month are adorable. They are 5" to 5.5" high and porcelain. Each of the boys has on a different set of clothing and are holding something pertaining to the season/month. The detail on these guys is outstanding, and I believe them to be the first complete boy series Lefton produced. They are found in the following Lefton catalogs: 1964, 1965 Spring and Summer, 1967-68 and 1973-74.

February boy is on his way to a slope with his skis, 5". Sticker used 1953-71. $40-45. *Courtesy of Matthew Roswell.*

January boy is ready for the new year with his horn and clock, 5". Sticker used 1953-71. $40-45.

March boy is ready for kite flying on a windy day, 5.25". Sticker used 1960-83. $40-45.

April boy is prepared for rain with his umbrella, boots and rain coat, 5". Sticker used 1953-71. $40-45.

Proud June boy has graduated and has his diploma, 5". Sticker used 1953-71. $40-45.

May boy is working on a garden with shovel and carrot in hand, 5.5". Sticker used 1960-83. $40-45.

July boy is all dressed up in top hat and coat, with his flag and fireworks, 5". $40-45. *Courtesy of Joe Goodsite.*

Markings on July boy. Sticker used 1960-83.

August boy is going on a picnic with a basket and his puppy, 5". Sticker used 1953-71. $40-45.

It's Halloween time and October boy is ready in his witch costume with a pumpkin and broom, 5". Sticker used 1953-71.

December is here and he's ready to play Santa, in his black boots and Santa suit, with a bag full of toys, 5". Sticker used 1953-71.

September is back to school for this boy with an apple and his school books, 5". Sticker used 1953-71. $40-45.

It's November and this boy is ready for Thanksgiving with his turkey and corn stalk, 5.5". Sticker used 1953-71. *Courtesy of Kyle Neiding.*

Siamese pair, 9", #1176. These were found in a Lefton' s undated catalog from the 1950s. They were also sold in 12" pairs, #1175. 9" pair sold for $2.50. 12" pair sold for $5.00. They came in four colors, green, black, pink or white. $250-260 pair.

Bisque Grandpa and Grandma, 6", #2571. $50-55.

Colorful porcelain boy and girl with bagpipes, 6", #3930. $50-55 pair.

Markings on bagpipe kids. Sticker used 1960-83.

Bottom markings on Grandpa and Grandma. Stamp used 1955-present. Sticker used 1962-90.

Angel gal and devil guy, porcelain. Removable pitchfork. This couple was found in an undated Lefton catalog from the 1950s. There were three different poses. All are #1055 and 3.25" high. $65-70.

Markings on bottom of the girl. These same markings are on the boy plus a sticker. Sticker used 1960-83.

St. Patrick's Day bisque couple, found in the 1974-75 Lefton catalog. 4", #KW4461. $35-40 pair.

Provincial couple with geese at their feet, 7.5", #6988. Sticker used 1962-90. $120-125.

Bottom markings on Edward. Stamp used 1955-present.

Bisque Colonial couple, Mildred and Edward, 8.5", #KW345. When produced, some of these didn' t have the names Mildred and Edward on the bottoms. $175-180 pair.

Fruit Fantasia

Fruit Fantasia is numbered in the 6700s and there are sixteen items to be found in Lefton's 1973 and 1974 catalogs. This pattern, as with the Mushroom Forest seems to be a kitchen pattern and not a serving pattern as there are no dinner or salad plates, bowls, cups or saucers listed that can be found in the catalogs. Due to the white background with light green shading and colorful fruit, this pattern will compliment any kitchen decor. Stickers found on most of these items were used 1960-83.

Large salt and pepper shakers, 6.25", #6754. $18-20.

Three-piece canister set shown here. Originally they came in a set of four, with sizes ranging from 10" down to 5.5", #6721. $100-110, four-piece set.

Cookie jar, 12", #6724. $55-60.

Cream and sugar, 3.5" and 4.5", #6756. $25-30.

Large milk pitcher, 7", #6724. $30-35.

Napkin holder, 5", #6728. $20-25.

Bottom marks on pitcher and bowl. Sticker used 1960-83.

Pitcher and bowl, 5.5", #6726. $35-40.

Green Holly (Hollyberry)

This pattern is highly collectible in today's secondary market and is called Green Holly by collectors. However, in Lefton's 1967-68 catalog, this pattern is called Hollyberry with the following numbers: 158, 159, 161, 402, 717, 787, 1187, 2369, 1346-1349, 1351-1353, 1355, 1357, 1359, 2688, 2691-2696, and 2637. In Lefton's 1974-75 Holiday book, this pattern is called Green Holly with all numbers in the 6000s. The majority of these newer items appear to be a bit shinier and darker with an almost "opalescent" look to them. Whole table settings can be found in Green Holly/Hollyberry and brighten up any Christmas table.

Although I have not found this to be true of Green Holly/Hollyberry items, many of the other older Christmas pieces on the secondary market today are in mint condition with the exception of paint wear or "off rub". Due to the use of "cold paint", the paint is very easily chipped. These pieces can be repaired with a little touch-up paint of the right shades and colors to make them look like new.

Candy box with red bow on lid, 4" square and 7" high, #3752. $35-40.

Cup and saucer, 3.75" round cup and 6" saucer, #6017. 9" plate, #2048. $20-22 cup and saucer, $18-20 plate.

Lamp with candle, 8.5", #2694. $75-80.

Marks on bottom of candle lamp. Sticker used 1953-71.

Bottom marks on sleigh candle holders. Sticker used 1960-83.

Pair of sleigh candle holders, 3" long and 2" high, #1693. $30-35 pair.

Pair of Stag candle holders, 7.5", #1368. $145-150 pair.

Musical lamp with candle, 10", #2692. Sticker used 1953-71. $85-90. *Courtesy of Stuart Brown.*

6.5" round covered candy dish with red bow on lid, #159. $35-40.

Snack set, #1363. 9" plate and 3.75" cup. Sticker used 1960-83. $30-35.

Bell bank with red bow, #158, 5" high and 5" at base. This bank came in a 3" and a 5" size. $30-35, and $40-45.

Cookie jar, 7", #1359. Sticker used 1953-71. $100-110.

Boot planter or candy holder, #6037, 3.5". This boot also came in 5" size, #5185. $20-25 and $30-35.

Bottom marks on boot planter. This black sticker seems to be found on only Christmas items, mostly Green Holly. Dated 1970/71.

This picture shows two different size sleighs. Actually, according to the Lefton catalogs, these sleighs came in three sizes. 10", #2637, 8", #1346 and 5", #4621. $60-65, $45-50 and $25-30.

Pair of 4" reindeer in two poses. Left, #1187, sticker used 1953-71. Right, #6004, black sticker used probably from 1960-83. Date on bottom of #6004 is 1970-71. The older one is a lighter green shade than the newer, as were most of the pieces produced in this time frame. The little reindeer are extremely popular today and not so easy to find in mint condition. $60-65 each.

Group picture with the large sleigh and nine of the reindeer. As you can see, some of the deer are almost opalescent in coloring. These are the newer ones.

Celery dish, 12", #1348. $35-40.

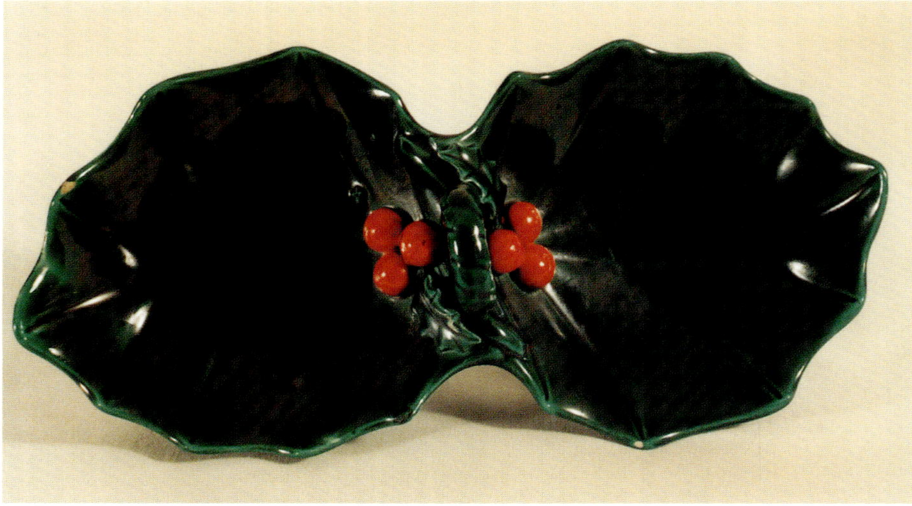

Two-compartment dish, 10", #1349. $30-35.

Large 8" vase, (also came in 5"), #5187. Have been unable to locate this vase in any of the Lefton catalogs I have available for research. $40-45.

Casserole dish, 9" round, #1364. Sticker used 1953-71. $60-65.

Four-compartment dish, 9.5", #1352. Sticker used 1953-71. $35-40.

Three-compartment dish, 9", #6009. Black sticker. $35-40.

Hands

Bottom marks on hand dish. Stamp used 1946-53.

Single white hand dish with applied pink roses, green leaves and gold trim, 5", no number. $40-45.

Lipstick holder, bisque with applied pink and blue flowers, green leaves, pink painted nails and gold trim. 5", #KW2933. Stamp used 1955-present. $25-30.

Porcelain ring dish with pink and blue Forget Me Not flowers and gold sponge trim, 4". $30-35.

Bottom markings on ring dish. This red sticker is the very largest one, but as you can see the wording is like the one used from 1953-71. I have found several of these. (See chapter on Markings)

Porcelain hand dish with Forget Me Not pink and blue flowers, pink painted nails and sponge and gold trim. From research, it seems that most of the hands produced by Lefton were made in both pink and white. 5.5", with no number. Stamp used 1946-50. $40-45.

Large, pink porcelain double hand dish with applied pink roses, green leaves and gold sponge trim, 6", #717. Stamp used 1946-53. $65-70.

White double hand dish with applied pink roses, green leaves and gold sponge trim, 6.5", #RV714. Stamp used 1946-53. $65-70.

Hand holding vase in pink porcelain with applied pink roses, light green leaves, pink nails and a tiny pink rose bud for a ring. Gold sponge trim, 6", #207. Sticker used 1946-53. Stamp used 1949-64. $60-65.

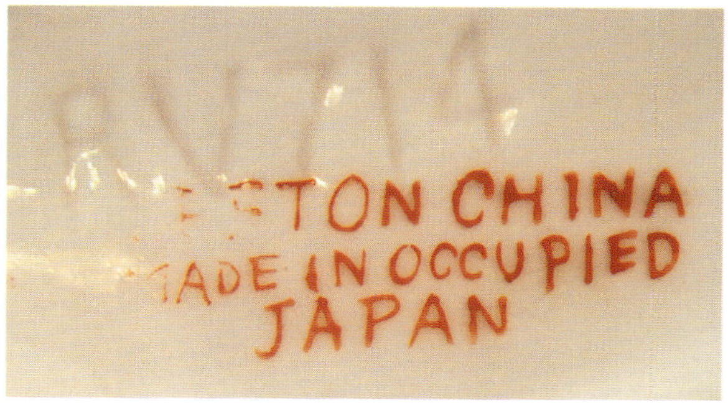

Bottom marking found on pink double hand dish. I have not seen this particular red stamp in any collector's books on Lefton China. A picture of this hand was found in an undated Lefton catalog from the 1950s, so it would have to be dated from 1946-53, which is the same date the Made in Occupied Japan stamp was used.

This pink hand is listed in a small blue collecting guide by Lefton from 1980. It isn't called a dish or ashtray, just hand, #717; the book says there were 68,772 produced from 1952-55. The original retail price was $1.20. The one pictured here is #717VP, 5" long. There are three markings on the bottom. One stamp was used 1946-53, and the Occupied Japan stamp was used 1946-53. It also has the large red sticker used from 1946-53. It's difficult to find a piece with three different markings. $45-50.

Pink (also was produced in white) hand vase with pink painted nails, applied pink rose, gold ring and gold sponge trim. 5", #152. Sticker used 1946-53. Stamp used 1946-50. $30-35.

Bottom markings on ring holder. Sticker used 1946-53. Stamp used 1946-50.

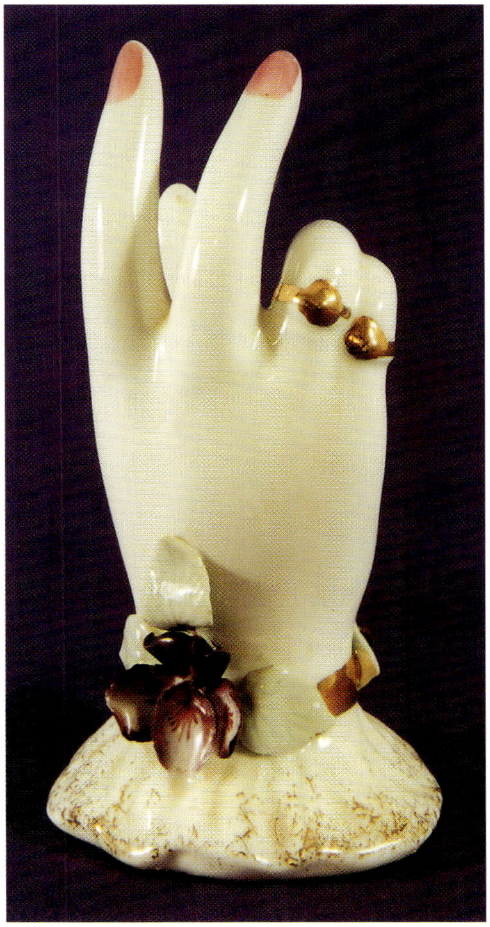

Pink porcelain ring holder, 4.5", with applied violet flower, light green leaves and gold sponge trim. #125, this ring holder hand is found in an undated Lefton catalog from the 1950s. At that time they sold for $7.20 per dozen. $40-45.

Pair of porcelain hands vase with pink, purple and blue Forget Me Not flowers, pink nails and gold sponge trim. 5", no number. Stamp used 1946-50. $55-60.

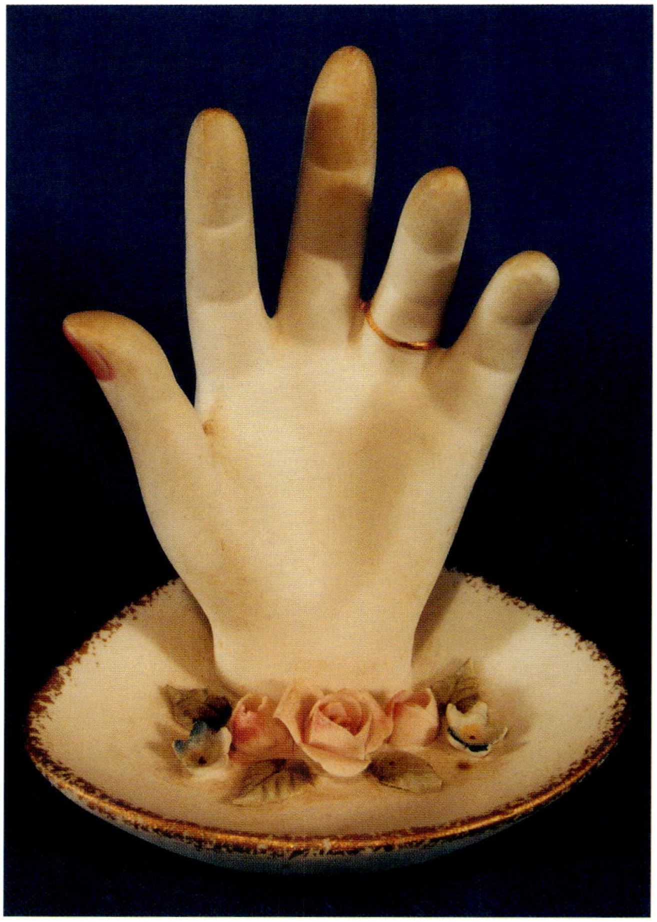

Hand ring holder, bisque with applied pink roses, blue Forget Me Nots, green leaves and gold sponge trim. 3.5", #1518. $20-25.

Bottom marks on ring holder. Sticker used 1946-53. Stamp used 1949-64.

Head Vases

In the old undated Lefton catalog from the 1950s, these vases were called "Hat Vases", not head vases, and were listed with Planters. The glossy porcelain finish was referred to as "glazed ceramic". Several of them in this catalog were named. "June", #042, #052 and #062 came in three sizes, 4.5", 5", and 7". Available colors were lavender, yellow and pink. "Barbara", #043, #053 and #063 also came in three sizes, 4.5", 5" and 5.5" and the same three colors. It seems the majority of these hat vases were produced in two or three sizes and colors. "Elaine", a fur-trimmed damsel, came in pink or green and sizes 5.25" and 7".

White porcelain lady with applied yellow roses and green leaves with gold trim, 5". No number. $90-95.

Porcelain lady wearing gold brimmed hat with scarf, green gloves and pearl earrings. Beautiful open eyes, 6", #4596. $85-90.

Bottom mark on lady with pink hat. I have been unable to date this stamp that was used in the 1950s.

Bottom marks on lady #4596. Sticker used 1953-71.

Porcelain child graduate girl, 5.5", #609. Stamp used 1950 to at least 1970. Sticker used 1953-71. $75-80.

Porcelain lady head with yellow and gold trimmed shawl, 6", #5920. $90-95.

Girl head with straw hat, porcelain, applied pink rose. 6", #50414. $75-80.

Bottom markings on girl with straw hat. Sticker used 1950 to at least 70. Dated 1956.

Bottom marks on lady with shawl. Sticker used 1960-83.

Bottom marks on lady in large brimmed hat. Sticker used 1953-71.

Lady head/bust in porcelain, wearing large brimmed hat with applied roses, 6.5", #1343. $120-125. *Courtesy of Debbie Roswell.*

Bottom markings on teen girl. Sticker used 1946-53.

Teen girl with eyes closed, wearing a hat and an applied stone necklace, matte finish. 6", #2251. $110-120.

This lovely head is found in an undated Lefton catalog from the 1950s. She has no name, but came in three sizes, 4.5", 5" and 7" and numbered 441, 641 and 541. Colors were either pink or yellow. This one is 7" and #541 in pink, with an applied yellow rose and heavy black lashes and gold trim. She is one of Lefton's oldest. $110-120. *Courtesy of Patti Neiding.*

Bottom stamp on pink lady. This stamp dates back to the 1950s and is rarely seen.

Wide brimmed hat lady in light blue with thick black lashes and both hands and arms showing. 6", #2705. $90-95.

Matte finish lady with thick black lashes, applied earrings and loose pearl necklace. 6", #2356. Sticker used 1953-71. $85-90.

Bottom marks on lady in light blue. Sticker used 1953-71.

Lady in wide brimmed hat in light pink with thick black lashes and both hands and arms showing. 6", #2705. Identical to the one in light blue. $90-95.

Lovely porcelain lady in yellow with yellow daisy in hair and pearl necklace and earrings, 5". #6525. Sticker used 1953-71. $95-100.

Bottom marks on lady #2667. Sticker used 1953-71.

Lady in high gloss finish with pale blue hat , thick black lashes and applied pink rose, 5", #2667. $95-110.

Stamp on bottom of Dainty Miss head, used 1950 to at least 1970.

Unusual Dainty Miss head with high gloss finish and hand painted in dark green with pink applied flower. 5", #7797. $110-120.

Girl head with large brimmed hat and stripes, 6", #4361. Sticker used 1953-71. $65-70.

Jam Jars

White porcelain with gold trim, handles and underplate, decorated in hand painted flowers. 5.5" long, #4668. $25-30.

Strawberry and Daisy, porcelain, 5", #H4898B. $25-30.

Bottom marks on flowered jam jar. Sticker used 1960-83. Stamp used 1955-present.

Bottom marks for Strawberry and Daisy jam jar. Sticker used 1960-83.

Porcelain yellow pear on a green leaf, with green leaf on lid, 4.5", #1071. Sticker used 1953-71. $35-40.

Bottom markings for Pixie/Elf jar. Sticker used 1946-53.

Pixie/Elf with large eyes and hat for lid, 5", #3971. $75-80.

Very unusual jam or condiment dish with four sections and four tiny spoons. (Spoons are not pictured). White porcelain with colorful fruit on the top of the lid, measuring 5" high and 5.5" across. #4682. Stamp used 1955-present. $50-55.

Brown jug jammer with basket weave bottom, 5", #H5070. $20-25.

Bottom marks for brown jug. Sticker used 1960-83.

Misty Rose, 3.5". No number. $40-45.

Bottom mark for Misty Rose jar. I am not sure when this stamp was used. There are two similar stamps used from 1953-75 and from 1968 to present. This looks to be a combination of both.

Della Robbia jar, 5", #1958. $25-30.

Burlap type jam jar, white porcelain with fruit lid, 5", #3906. $20-25.

Bottom marks on burlap jar. Sticker used 1953-71. Uncommon stamp, date unknown.

Miss Priss

An adorable little blue cat face, the Miss Priss items are very highly sought after on the secondary market today. She is shown in several of the Lefton catalogs beginning in the 1960s. The 1964 catalog shows nine items. Teabag holder #1506, salt and pepper shakers #1511, pitcher #1504, sugar and creamer #1508, teapot #1516, cookie jar #1502, two compartment dish #1507, covered butter dish #1505 and jam jar #1515. In this catalog it says that the pitcher and teabag holder were discontinued. Lefton's 1965 catalog shows the sugar and creamer, teapot, cookie jar, salt and pepper shakers and the jam jar. Also included is a baby set with bowl and mug #3553. Shown in Lefton's 1967-68 catalog are salt and pepper shakers, jam jar, sugar and creamer, teapot, cookie jar baby set and a planter #3860. The 1973 catalog pictures the cookie jar, salt and pepper shakers and the teapot.

Jam jar with underplate, #1515, 4.5". $80-85.

Teabag holder, #1506, 3". $50-55.

Pair of egg cups, #1510, 2.5". $65-70 each.

Cookie jar, #1502, 7.5". $200-210. *Courtesy of Patti Neiding.*

Bottom marks on cookie jar. Sticker used 1960-83.

Teapot, six-cup, #1516, 6.5". $210-220.

Only bottom mark found on teapot. No sticker.

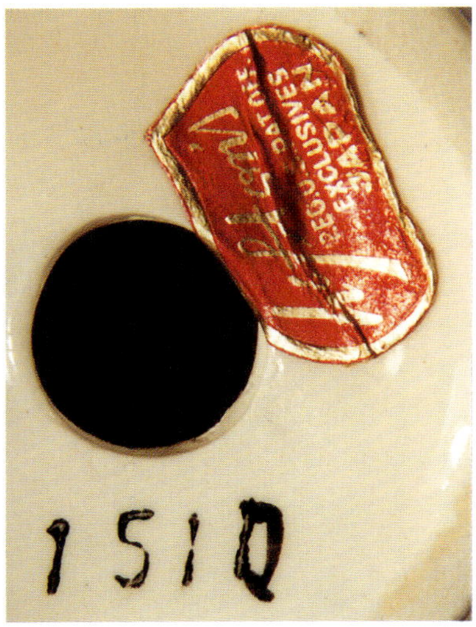

Bottom marks on salt and pepper shakers. This sticker was used 1953-71.

Salt and pepper shakers, #1510, 3". $50-55.

Cream and sugar, #1508, 4". *Courtesy of Mildred Urban.* $80-85.

Bottom marks on sugar bowl. Sticker used 1960-83.

5.5" spoon rest with 3" shaker, #1525. I've had several collectors ask me if this is an egg holder and not a spoon rest. In Lefton's catalogs, these are called spoon rests. I just wanted to clarify that. This item is not pictured in any of the catalogs we have researched. $95-100.

Bottom markings on spoon rest with shaker. Sticker used 1946-53.

Grouping of Miss Priss items, including a cookie jar, sugar and creamer, salt and pepper, covered butter dish, jam jar with underplate, teapot and teabag holder. *Courtesy of Pam Sanders.*

Milk pitcher, #1504, 6". *Courtesy of Pam Sanders.*

Spoon Rest, #1524, 6". *Courtesy of Pam Sanders.*

Cup, 4", #1503. *Courtesy of Pam Sanders.*

Covered butter dish, #1505, 6.5".*Courtesy of Pam Sanders.*

Mushroom Forest

The Mushroom Forest pattern is found in the 1973 catalog. Twenty one items are pictured with most of the numbers in the 6000s. This was an extremely popular pattern and color in the 1970s and it appears that it's popularity is coming back. I have noticed the price climbing this past year on this series, on auctions and at Antique malls. Dinnerware, such as place settings apparently were not produced. The catalogs show nothing in plates, cups, saucers or bowls.

Most of the Mushroom Forest series has the following black stamp. This stamp was used from 1950 to at least 1970.

Gravy boat/sauce dish with underplate, 7" long, #6465. $40-45.

Bottom markings on gravy boat/sauce dish. Stamp used 1950 to at least 1970. This silver paper label is one not seen very often, but it is on several of the Mushroom Forest items I have.

Cart planter measuring 5" long and 4" high, #6360. $30-35.

Covered dish, 7" high, #6477. $35-40.

Basket with handle, 4", #6473. $20-25.

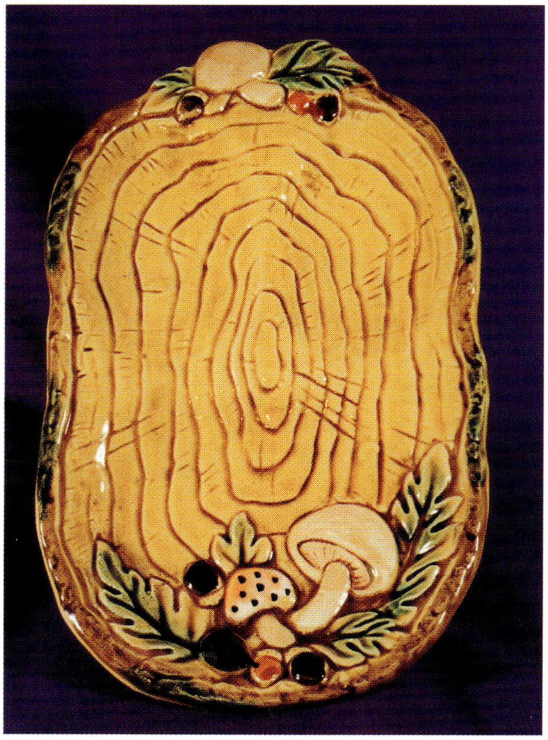

Double spoon rest, 8" long, #6357. $30-35.

Round pedestal planter, 3.5" high by 6"round, #6471. $30-35.

Bottom marks on spoon rest. Stamp used 1950 to at least 1970.

Egg plate for 12 eggs, 12" long, #6354. $40-45.

Jam jar with glass spoon, 5.5", #6353. $40-45

Napkin holder, 5", #6360. $20-25.

Covered butter dish, 7.5" long, #6468. $25-30.

Four-piece canister set, sizes ranging from 9" down to 5.5", #6353. $100-110.

To date, I'm still not sure about this teapot. It has the same sticker as the rest of the mushroom pieces, but there is no black Lefton stamp, just the black stamped #3301 and the sticker used 1960-83. Note the difference of pattern change with the mushrooms on top. All the others have the large white or gold mushroom on top. This one is orange with the black dots and there is no large white or gold mushroom. Also, around the bottom is a little different and the coloring is a shade lighter. Either the factory changed the style a bit or this is not a Lefton piece. $45-50.

Two-compartment plate, 8" by 12", #6339. $25-30.

Large salt and peppers, 6.5", #6355. $20-25.

4" Coffee mugs, #6356. $15-18 each.

Tureen, four pieces, 10" x 10", #6464. $100-110.

Pitcher and bowl set, 5.5", #6469. $45-50.

Pair of pitcher and bowl wall pockets, 6.5", #7068. $45-50.

Bottom marks on wall pockets.

Cookie Jar, 10.5", #6359. $70-75.

Pearlized/Opalescent Items

Angel in pink gown with pink flower necklace, gold trim and spaghetti trim on head, 4", #1478. $40-45.

Large 7" white cat bank with beautiful glass eyes, #1566. Sticker used 1953-71. $40-45.

Angel in pink gown with blue flower necklace, gold trim and spaghetti trim on head, 4", #1478. $40-45.

Bottom marks on both pink and blue flowered angels. Sticker used 1953-71.

Pixie/elf sitting on a pointed shoe planter with applied Forget Me Not pink and blue flowers and spaghetti type leaves. 7" long and 4" high, #50478. Sticker used 1953-71. $40-45.

Large 8" long by 6" high pink pig bank with applied pink roses, green leaves, and beautiful eye detail. #2814, these pigs came in at least two sizes. The smaller one is 6" long by 4" high and is #2813. $35-40 for large size, $25-30 for small size.

Pink standing dog with applied pink and blue Forget Me Not flowers, spaghetti type spotted fur, and rhinestone eyes. 7", #871. Sticker used 1953-71. $30-35.

Pixie/Elf sitting on covered wagon planter with applied pink and blue Forget Me Not flowers with spaghetti type leaves. 7" long and 5" high, #2363. $40-45.

Pink deer with applied pink and blue Forget Me Not flowers, applied blue rhinestone eyes and spaghetti type trim, 7", #YU871. $30-35.

Bottom mark on covered wagon planter. There is also a sticker, used 1953-71.

Pixie/Elf sitting on watering can/planter with pink and blue applied Forget Me Not flowers, spaghetti type leaves and gold trim. 8" long and 5" high, #50479. $40-45.

Cat figurine with blue applied rhinestone eyes, pink and blue Forget Me Not flowers, and spaghetti type trim. 6", #YU590. Sticker used 1953-71. $25-30.

Large Pixie/Elf planter with adorable facial detail, 7" long and 5" high, #4557. Sticker used 1953-71. $40-45.

Four footed planter with Pixie/Elf. This one has wings on her back. Pink applied flowers with green spaghetti type leaves, 5", #2703. $45-50.

Bottom markings on boot planter. ESD Canadian import, Japan stamp and red and gold sticker.

Boot planter with Pixie/Elf laying on the toe in a green and white outfit and hat with gold shoes. 5.5" long and 4" high, #22893. $35-40.

Pair of Pixie/Elf planters with rabbit, applied pink and blue Forget Me Not flowers, spaghetti type leaves and gold trim. 4.5" high, #50480. $40-45 each.

8" cat figurine with applied blue rhinestone eyes, pink and white Forget Me Not flowers, and spaghetti type fur trim. #YU590. There are two styles of this cat with the same number. Sticker used 1953-71. $30-35.

Bottom markings on planters with rabbits. Sticker used 1953-71.

Pixie/Elf wheelbarrow planter with pink and blue applied Forget Me Not flowers. 5" high by 6" long, #1685. Sticker used 1953-71. $40-45.

Pitchers and Bowls

Bottom marks on Elegant Rose set. Stamp used 1955-present.

Elegant Rose set with gold trim, 3.5", #6328. $25-30.

Green Heritage floral set with gold trim. This set came in at least two sizes. 4", #4577, $40-45. 5.25", #5478, $60-65.

Bottom markings for Green Heritage set. Stamp used 1955-present. Sticker used 1962-90.

Large Aster pitcher and bowl set with white background. Pitcher is 5.5" high, bowl is 6.5" round. Sticker used 1960-83. $35-40.*Courtesy of Debbie Roswell.*

Off-white background with spring flowers and gold trim, pitcher and bowl. 3.5", #696. $20-25.

Bottom markings for set #696. Stamp used 1955-present. Sticker used 1962-90.

Brown Heritage floral set, 4", #1872. $40-45. *Courtesy of Debbie Roswell.*

Bottom markings for #2008. Sticker used 1962-90. Stamp used 1955-present.

This is a pattern I have not been able to find in any of the catalogs I have on hand for research. All-white background with green and gold trim and tiny pink flowers. 4", #2008. $30-35.

Spring Flowers set, shiny white with gold trim, 4". #6843. $45-50.

Bottom marks for Spring Flowers set. Sticker used 1960-83. Stamp used 1955-present.

Planters

Animals and Birds

White porcelain matte finish poodle, 8", #H7859. $40-45.

Bottom mark on poodle. Sticker didn' t show in picture, used 1953-71.

Pink porcelain cat with closed eyes, spaghetti fur and gold sponge trim, 5", #126. Sticker used 1946-53. $55-60.

Porcelain mouse, bluish/green in color with spaghetti hair and gold trim, 6" long by 8" wide, #KB351. Sticker used 1953-71. $40-45.

Very colorful white goose in hand painted porcelain. 8" high and 7" long at base, #4124. Sticker used 1960-83. $30-35.

Brown and black donkey, 7", #H7702. Sticker used 1960-83. $45-50.

Pink poodle planter with spaghetti fur, applied white flowers and leaves and gold trim, 5". #1632. $35-40.

Bottom marks on poodle. Sticker used 1953-71.

Gray and white porcelain cat with glass eyes, 7", #H4625. Sticker used 1960-83. $35-40.

Large pink and gray porcelain elephant, 10" long, #366. Sticker used 1953-71. $35-40.

10.5" Lady wearing a hat and a white dress with dark pink flowers, #499B. This lovely lady is porcelain and was produced in two different flower colors, the other being blue. $80-85.

Bottom marks for lady #499B. Sticker used 1953-71.

Lady in olive green dress holding a fan, 8", #4599. Sticker used 1953-71. $60-65.

Bottom markings on large lady planter. Sticker used 1953-71.

This is perhaps the largest lady planter I have ever seen. She measures 10.5" high, wears a dress and wide brimmed hat in brown tones, and carries a basket of flowers. The detail is remarkable on this lady. #2790B. $100-110.

This is Olive, a porcelain lady planter with an apron full of vegetables, 6", #1685B. $55-60.

Bottom markings on Olive. Sticker used 1953-71.

Porcelain young girl in a dark pink dress holding a fan, #1533. Sticker used 1953-71. $35-40

We don't see too many of the gentlemen planters. This one is 7" high and standing in front of a fence. Matte finish, #3075. $60-65.

Bottom markings on both the lady and the gentleman. Sticker used 1953-71. This black stamp was most likely used in the 1950s.

This lady apparently goes with the gentleman as the numbers and the stamps are the same on both. Matte finish, 7" and #3075. $50-55.

Bottom marks on burgundy lady. Stamp used 1950 to at least 1970. Dated 1957.

Beautiful porcelain lady with burgundy hat and dress with applied flowers, carrying a parasol. 8.5", #164. $55-60.

Mr. Toodle type white puppies with applied pink flowers on heads, 3.5", #1726. $20-25.

Bottom marks on white puppies. Sticker used 1953-71.

Fruit Fantasia set, 6.5", #6754. $18-23.

One of Lefton's most popular series is this Blue Bird! 3.5", #282, $40-45.

Dancing Leaves shakers, 6", #7277. $18-23.

Yellow owls with big green-trimmed eyes, 3", #H6836. $20-25.

Bottom mark on owls. Sticker used 1960-83.

Pink porcelain elephants with applied flowers and stones and gold trim. 2.5", #H458 . $25-30.

Bottom marks on elephants. On one there is the oval red and gold Japan sticker and the number. On the other is the number and the sticker used 1953-71.

Onion set, 2" high and 3" round. No number. Sticker used 1946-53. $30-35

Porcelain kittens in sprinkling cans, 3.5", #2074. Sticker used 1953-71. $20-25.

Brown horse heads, 3", #H01. Sticker used 1953-71. $25-30.

Bee Line set, 3", #1288. $20-25.

Bottom marks on Bee Line set. Oval red and gold Japan sticker with the number on one, and the sticker used 1960-83 and the number on the other.

Saucers, Cups and Snack Sets

Bottom mark for Bone China set. No number. Date is unknown on this stamp.

English Bone China cup and saucer, white background with roses and gold trim. 3". $30-35.

Small elf/pixie mug with handle, white porcelain with adorable little face. These were also produced in red. 3", #3545. $35-40.

Bottom markings on elf/pixie mug. Sticker used 1953-71. Stamp used in the 1950s.

Bottom marks for Green Heritage set. Stamp used 1955-present.

Green Heritage floral snack set, 8", #3071. $30-35.

White porcelain cup and saucer with gray and green flowers and gold trim, 4". No number. $30-35.

Bottom marks for cup and saucer. Stamp used 1946-50. Sticker used 1946-53.

Bottom mark for yellow snack set. Stamp used 1946-50.

Yellow snack set with yellow roses, green leaves and gold trim, 8", #2759. $30-35.

Bottom markings for black cup and saucer. Stamp used 1946-52.

Beautiful black porcelain cup and saucer, white inside with gold angels and trim, #20583. $50-55.

Yellow tulip pedestal mug, white porcelain with yellow and green trim. 4.5", #7124. Sticker used 1960-83. $12-15.

Bottom marks for Cherry Blossom set. Stamp used 1949-55.

Cherry Blossom white with gold trim snack set, 8", #884. $40-45.

Bottom markings for Soldier mug. Stamp used 1955-present. Sticker used 1953-71.

Civil War Soldier mug with sword for handle, 4.5" high, #KW1112. $50-55.

Dainty Miss cup and saucer. Cup is 3.25" high, saucer is 6.25" round, #936. $90-95.

Smoking Related Items

Bottom markings on pink ashtray. Sticker used 1946-53. Stamp used 1946-50.

Pink porcelain ashtray with Forget Me Not pink and blue flowers and gold sponge trim, 5" long. #40454. $30-35.

Bottom markings on duck ashtray set. Canadian import with the ESD Japan stamp and sticker.

Cigarette box with two ashtrays, porcelain. The box has an applied duck on the top. The duck on the ashtrays is hand painted. Box is 2" by 5", #HP7160. $25-30. *Courtesy of Rick Osborn.*

Large ashtray measuring 12" by 7.5" with hand painted tower scene and gold sponge trim, #1623. $35-40.

Marks on bottom of large ashtray. Sticker used 1953-71.

Blue Paisley ashtrays and holder, five-piece set, 3" square, #2343. $20-25.

Leaf-shaped bisque ashtray with bird, 6" long, #KW1240. These ashtrays came in several different bird patterns. $25-30.

Bottom marks on bird ashtray. Stamp used 1955-present. There are three ashtrays similar to this shown in an undated Lefton catalog from the 1950s, except the leaf shape and numbers are different. Numbers in catalog are 4014, 4015 and 4016.

Six-piece smoking set with hand painted Pheasants. Covered box, four ashtrays and a lighter. Box is 4" by 3.5". Lighter is 3" high. $50-55. *Courtesy of Ray Osborn.*

Bottom stamp for six-piece smoking set. Stamp used 1949-64.

Double stamped bottom marks on pink ashtray. Multicolored stamp used 1946-50. Black stamp used 1950 to at least 1970.

Odd-shaped pink porcelain ashtray with applied pink flowers and gold trim, 5" long, #KW4700. $30-35. *Courtesy of Jill Vassmer.*

Rose Chintz set with two ashtrays and box with lid, 5" long by 3.5" wide, #788R. Stamp used 1949-64. $45-50.

Pink porcelain swan ashtray with applied gold flowers and gold trim, 3" long, #954C. $20-25.

Bottom stamp on swan ashtray. Stamp used 1946-50.

Bottom marks for swan ashtray. Stamp was used 1946-50. The black Japan stamp by itself is seldom seen.

Pink porcelain swan ashtray with applied yellow, blue and pink flowers and gold sponge trim. 5.5" long. These were produced in three sizes, this being the largest. #954A, #954B and #954C. Pictured in Lefton's undated catalog from the 1950s. $30-35.

White oval porcelain ashtray with bird, applied flowers and leaves and gold sponge trim. 5" long, #262. Pictured in an undated Lefton catalog from the 1950s. $50-55.

White porcelain sleigh ashtray with applied pink roses, green leaves and gold sponge trim, 3.5" long. No number. $95-100. *Courtesy of Sara Selander*

Bottom stamp on sleigh ashtray. Stamp used 1946-50.

Pink ashtray with gold sponge trim, applied pink roses and green leaves, and bird, 5" long. No number. Stamp used 1946-50. $50-55.

Vases

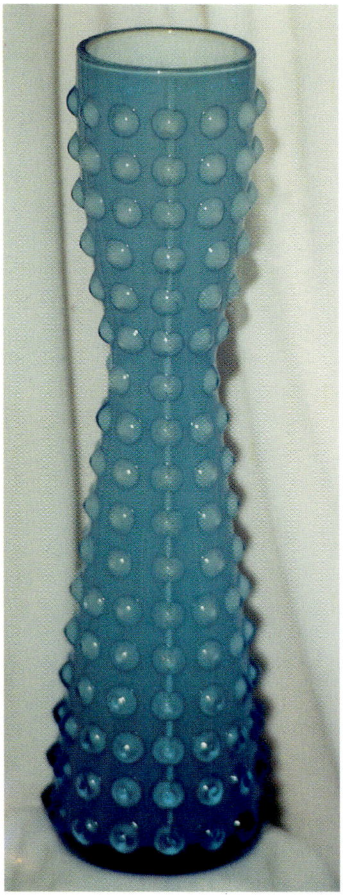

Hobnail bud vase, blue cased with white, 9", #7102. Has round black and gold sticker on bottom. I have no dating on this sticker. It is found on most of the glass vases. *Courtesy of Stuart Brown.*

Three glass vases, blue, green, and red, sizes 9", 8.5" and 7" with black round sticker. $25-30 each. *Courtesy of Stuart Brown.*

Green hobnail-cased glass vase, 9" #7102. $25-30. *Courtesy of Stuart Brown.*

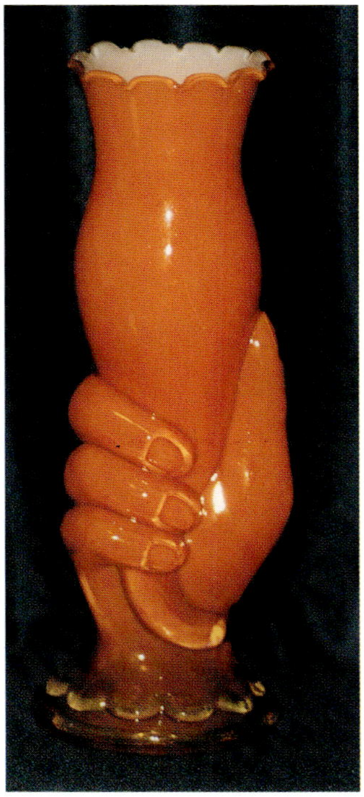

Lovely orange glass hand vase, 8.75", #7725. $40-45. *Courtesy of Stuart Brown.*

10" purple glass vase, #3222. Found in Lefton's 1964 catalog. Sticker used 1953-71. $30-35. *Courtesy of Stuart Brown.*

Green hobnail bud vase cased with white, 9", #7102. $25-30. *Courtesy of Stuart Brown.*

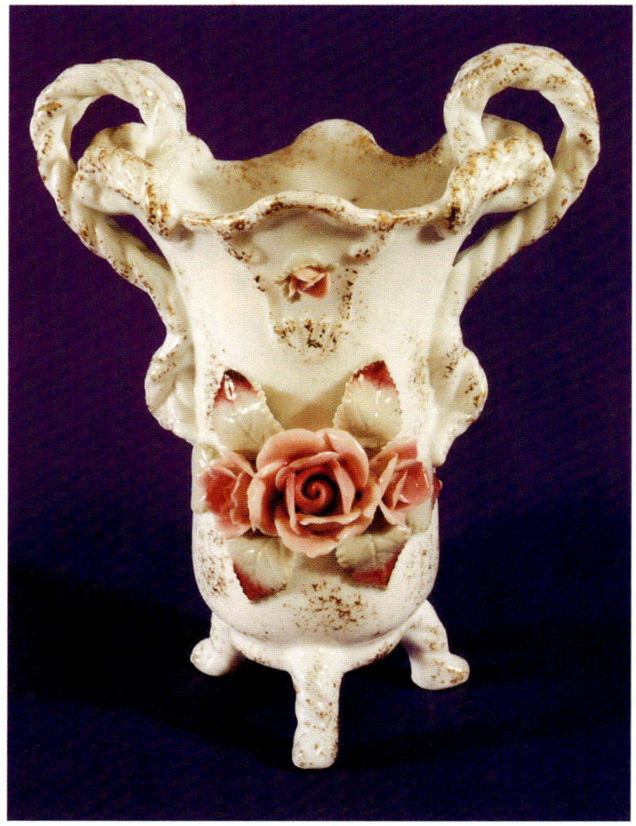

White glossy porcelain vase with applied pink roses, leaves and gold sponge trim, 6", #089. $55-60.

Bottom marks on white vase. Stamp used 1946-50.

Bisque Boutique vase found in Lefton's 1974-75 Holiday Catalog, 6", #7904. Stamp used 1955-present. $20-25.

Bottom markings on Lily of the Valley vase. Stamp used 1946-50.

Pink porcelain vase with Lily of the Valley applied flowers and leaves with gold sponge trim, 6", #124. I believe this same vase came in a miniature, 3", with possibly the same number. $50-55 for the 6".

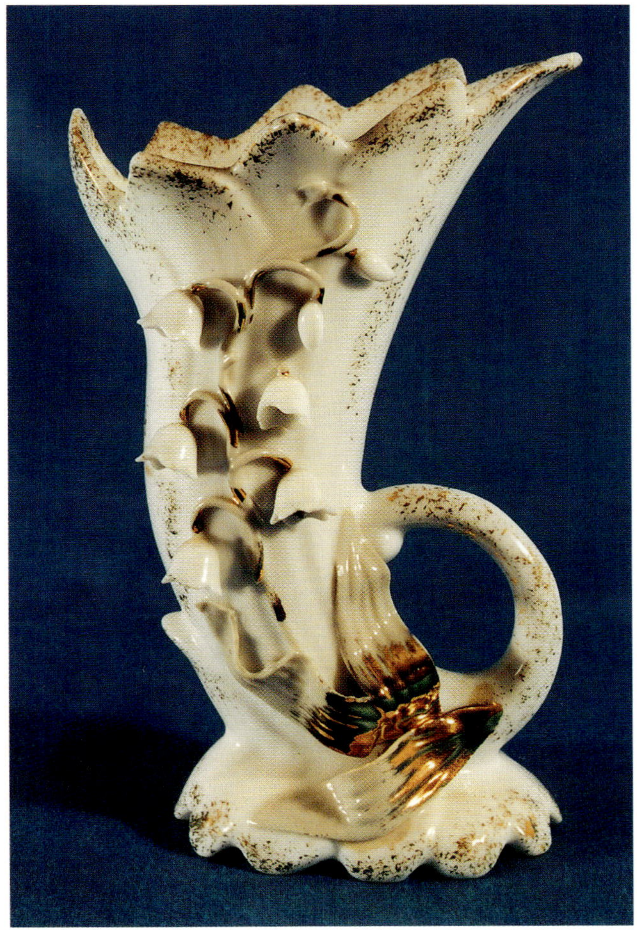

White porcelain cornucopia vase with applied Lily of the Valley flowers and gold sponge trim. These came as a pair, 6.5", #282. Stamp used 1946-50. $80-85 pair.

Pair of pink 6" porcelain pitcher vases with applied fruit and leaves, gold handles and gold sponge trim. Shown is the front and back side. $40-45 each.

Bottom markings on pitcher vases. Multicolored stamp used 1946-50. Black stamp used 1950 to at least 1970. Sticker used 1946-53. Unusual with double stamps.

White bisque-handled vase with applied flowers and gold trim, 6.5", #KW8021. $45-50.

Bottom marks on white bisque vase. Stamp used 1955-present. Sticker used 1962-90.

Green Heritage floral ewer, 5.5", #748. Stamp used 1955-present. $40-45. *Courtesy of Stuart Brown.*

Pair of pink porcelain vases with applied Forget Me Not flowers, side handles and gold trim. 6", #70459. $90-95 pair.

Bottom marks on pair of pink vases. Stamp used 1946-50. Sticker used 1946-53.

White porcelain stein vase with applied pink roses, green leaves and gold trim. 7", #7074. Sticker used 1946-53. Stamp used 1946-53. $60-65. *Courtesy of Stuart Brown.*

6" white porcelain vase with applied pink roses, green leaves, gold handle and gold sponge trim. #7075. $50-55. *Courtesy of Stuart Brown.*

Pair of bisque cornucopia vases, pastel in color and decorated with applied pink roses, 6", #774. $90-100 pair.

Bottom markings on cornucopia vases. Stamp used 1946-50.

Pink bisque vase with applied flowers, leaves and gold trim, 4", #1847. $20-25.

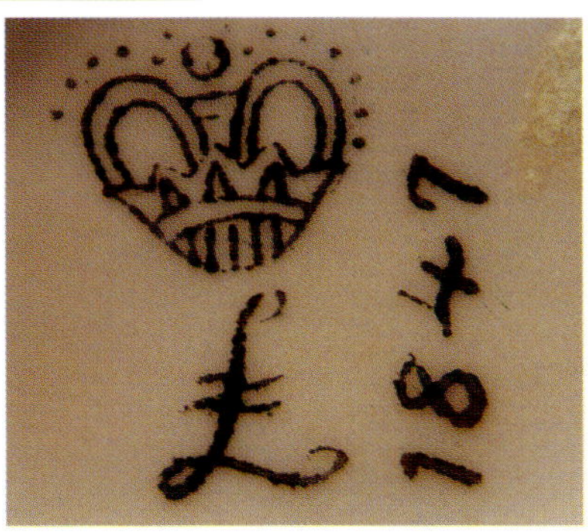

Bottom marks on pink vase. Sticker used 1968 (unsure).

Pair of Brown Heritage floral vases with gold handles, 5" and 5.5", #2763. Sticker used 1960-83. $40-45 each.

Black dull finish porcelain black cat with pink ears, applied spaghetti type fur trim, rhinestone eyes and gold bow. 8", no number. $40-45.

Bottom markings on black cat. Stamp used 1950 to at least 1970. Sticker used 1946-53.

An arrangement of miniature vases from the collection of Stuart Brown, ranging from 3-3.5". Pricing on these vary, according to style. With applied flowers and fruit, $25-30. Plain with nothing applied, $18-23 each.

Pair of pink porcelain bag vases with applied pink and blue Forget Me Not flowers and gold sponge trim, 4.5", no numbers. Stamp used 1946-50. $65-70 for pair.

Wall Hangings/Pockets

Out of all the Lefton wall hangings I have seen, these are my personal favorites. Antique white oval wood frames with hangers at the top and gold trim. They have a dark green felt background. A pair of angels were attached by wires. The backs are covered and look like they are original, so I'm sure they came from the factory like that, although I have never found them in any Lefton catalog. The frames are 7.5", the angels are 3.5". They both have #2476 on the backs and the sticker on them was used 1953-71. $100-110 pair. These may be considered rare.

Colorful love birds wall pocket, 8", #H7446. $35-40.

Markings on love birds pocket. Sticker used 1960-83.

Early American Rooster match holder, 6.25", #2102. Sticker used 1953-71. $40-45.

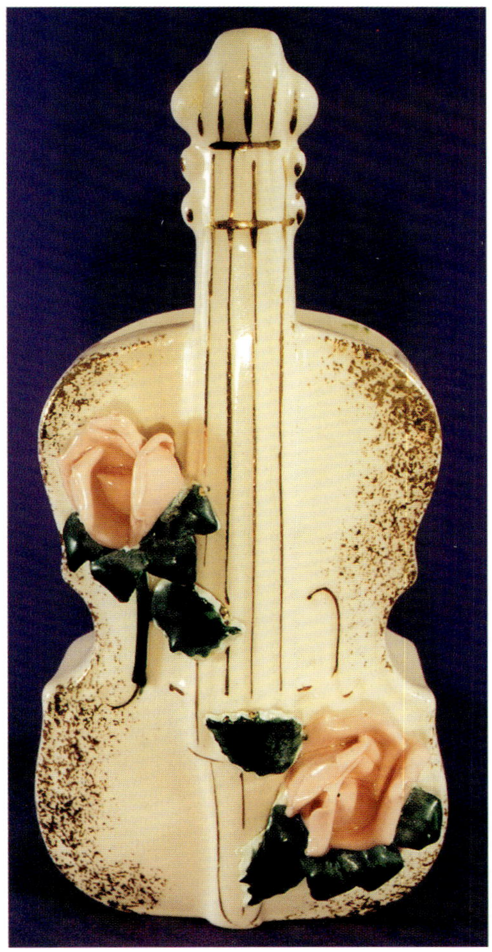

Wall pocket with applied large pink roses, green leaves and gold sponge trim, 7", #212. Sticker used 1946-53. $55-60

Pair of duck wall pockets, 5", #50575. Sticker used 1946-53. $60-65 for pair. *Courtesy of Rick Osborn.*

Bottom marks on deer pockets. I have been unable to find any dating for this black, round stamp. Sticker was used 1946-53.

Pair of black deer wall pockets with spaghetti and gold trim, gold bows and rhinestone eyes, 6" high. The white back pocket is shiny porcelain, but the deer are a very dull, black finish. No number. $45-50 each.

Porcelain pair of girl wall pockets with fans, 7", #2934. $100-110 pair.

Bottom marks on girl wall pockets with fans. Sticker used 1946-53.

Blue Cat with red bow wall pocket, 5.5", #150. This cat was found in an undated Lefton catalog from the 1950s and came in pink or blue glazed china. At that time they sold for $6.00 per dozen. $65-70.

Sweet little girl head wall pocket, porcelain with lovely eyes, 5", # 4794. Sticker used 1946-53. $80-85.

Oval bisque wall plaques with applied Colonial couple, 10" high, #5826. $100-110 pair.

Old-fashion man and woman porcelain wall plates with white background and gold trim, 4", #1241. $35-40 pair.

Back stamp on both plates. Stamp used 1946-50.

Back markings on angel plaques. Sticker used 1960-83.

Very ornate pair of angel wall plaques. Hand painted in dark green and gold, 8", #5487. $45-50 pair. *Courtesy of Joyce Benson.*

Hand painted winter scene on white porcelain with gold trim, wall hanging, 8.5", #588. $20-25.

Hand painted summer scene on white porcelain with gold trim, wall hanging, 8.5", #588. $20-25.

Back markings on all three hand painted scene hangings. Sticker used 1962-90. Stamp used 1955-present.

Hand painted mountain scene on white porcelain with gold trim, wall hanging, 8.5", #588. $20-25.

Beautiful pair of white porcelain wall hangings, Only A Rose, 7.5" high, #4536. $80-85 pair.

Wall-hanging burlap style spoon rest, 5", #3909. $15-18.

Bottom mark for spoon rest. Stamp used 1950 through at least 1970.

Bibliography

George Zoltan Lefton Company. Catalogs issued to retail dealers for the purpose of buying and selling new items in Gift Stores, from the following years. Two undated catalogs, believed to be from the 1950s. Catalogs from 1964, 1965, 1967-68, 1973, 1974, 1974-75 Holiday Book, A Collectors Guide dated 1980, catalogs from 1986 and 1993. Lefton's General Office and Warehouse is located in Chicago, IL, 60609.

DeLozier, Loretta. *Collector's Encyclopedia of Lefton China, Book 2.* Paducah, Kentucky: Collector's Books, Schroeder Publishing Co., Inc. 1997.

Schneider, Mike. *The Complete Cookie Jar Book.* West Chester, Pennsylvania: Schiffer Publishing, Ltd. 1991.